Liz Halfpenny

GW01418640

Produced for the Politics Association

Old Hall Lane, Manchester M13 0XT

Sheffield Hallam University Press
Learning Centre
City Campus
Pond Street
Sheffield S1 1WB

First published 1996

Revised 1999

Designed and typeset by Design Studio, Learning Centre, Sheffield Hallam University

©1999   ISBN 0 86339 670 4

Sheffield Hallam University

WHAT IS POLITICS?

AN INTRODUCTION TO GCSE POLITICS

(Revised edition 1999)

COLIN PILKINGTON

Although this book can be treated as a general
introduction to the study of politics it is based on, and is
written to accompany, the GCSE Politics syllabus offered by

AQA - NEAB.

The author, Colin Pilkington, is an experienced senior
examiner in Politics at 16+ and is currently

Chief Examiner for GCSE Politics.

About the author:

Colin Pilkington has over twenty years experience of teaching and examining Government and Politics at all levels. For many years he was Head of Humanities and Social Studies at Ruffwood School on Merseyside. More recently he spent a year as guest lecturer in Political Sociology at the Liverpool Institute of Higher Education. Since 1975 he has been examiner, moderator and subject panel member for CSE, CEE and GCSE Government and Politics and is currently Chief Examiner in GCSE Politics for AQA-NEAB. As a writer he has published *Britain in the European Union Today* and a number of other works in the *British Politics Today* series for Manchester University Press, a book on *Issues in British Politics* for Macmillan and, as Fulcrum Publishing, has published a popular series of revision packs for A-level and GCSE Government and Politics.

CONTENTS

PREFACE
to the Revised Edition 1999.

A MESSAGE TO TEACHERS

During the winters of 1994/5 and 1995/6, my colleagues and I toured the country to meet teachers of GCSE Politics and brief them on the new syllabus and tiered examination that was due to be introduced by the NEAB in the summer of 1996. Everywhere we went we were greeted by the same *cri de coeur*, "What books are there that we could use as a teaching resource?" And the reply had to be that there was none. A small entry subject such as GCSE Politics is not viable for a commercial publisher who aims to sell a print order of 5000 texts, in class sets of 30 books at a time. In attempting to teach the subject most teachers have been thrown back on their own resources, mediating items taken from the newspapers, or interpreting A-level texts.

This little book was an attempt to respond to an obvious need: a need that was emphasised in the outcome of the first examination under the new syllabus. The manifest failure of many candidates to grasp such basic terminology as the meaning of 'select committee' or 'cabinet' emphasised the need for a basic primer that would contribute to improving our students' political literacy.

i

Although not exclusively for the use of GCSE students, this book is built around the current GCSE syllabus.

- The introduction attempts to explain 'what is politics?' by a simplified outline of political theory. Although it is situated first, as an introduction, there are some fairly complex concepts involved that may well be too advanced for the beginner, and it might be felt best just to glance at this section for the moment and to leave a closer examination until later in the course of study.

- Part one is sub-titled 'Politics and the Individual' and corresponds to part one of the syllabus - 'What is Politics?' This deals with an individual's participation in politics, from the committee structure of clubs and societies, through membership of pressure groups and political parties, to the question of elections and voting behaviour.

- Part two, sub-titled 'Structures and Processes', corresponds to parts two and three of the syllabus and covers, as the title suggests, the structures and processes of British government and politics, at local, national and European level.

- Part three, as implied in the title 'Political Issues', corresponds to part four of the syllabus. The issues are grouped together for convenience into economic issues, social issues, constitutional issues and so on. Of course, the term 'issues' is fairly vague since much of the study of politics can be said to be about issues. Here the term is taken to mean specifically those issues that become associated with party policy and thereby become instrumental in motivating voting behaviour.

- Part four is a purely practical section which includes advice on how the student should tackle the course work requirement, and an analysis of the type of questions that might be expected in the written examination, indicating the sort of responses that might be required.

Although it is safe to say that there will be nothing asked in the examination that is not mentioned in these pages, this book is obviously not enough in itself and should be used in association with normal classroom lessons, written exercises, discussions and coursework assignments. The student is also recommended to make full use of information to be gleaned from the press, broadcast media and Internet so as to keep up to date with the ever-changing world of political events.

The important terms and concepts are highlighted in the text by being printed in **bold** or *italics*, or by being <u>underlined</u>. The student would do well to learn by heart the meaning of words and phrases emphasised in this way. It might be thought useful for the student to build their own glossary of useful words and phrases, just as a language student will keep a vocabulary book. At the end of each chapter there is a question, or series of questions, intended to motivate readers to think for themselves, or to discuss the subject with their fellow student, or to suggest some exercises to clarify their political studies.

The need for a revised edition of the book became obvious after the European elections in June 1999. Much of what was written originally is still accurate and valid but there is a change of emphasis given that there has been a general election and a change of government since the first edition was issued. It is also true that in certain fields such as electoral reform, devolution and Europe there have been significant changes under the Blair government. While executing these changes in a new edition I have taken the opportunity of adding what has been pointed out to me repeatedly as being the one great lack of the first edition - and that is an index.

I should like to express my indebtedness to members of the Politics Association for their help and support in the writing of this book, and in particular to Duncan Watts as editor, to Glynis Sandwith of the Politics Association Resource Centre and to Monica Moseley of Sheffield Hallam University Press. My gratitude goes to those members of the secretariat of AQA-NEAB whose task it was to service the social science subjects. This is particularly true of Marilyn Ashworth, who was the subject officer who did most to get the new syllabus off the ground during the formative period, her work being substantially continued and assisted by Peter Ratcliffe and Russell Spencer. My thanks also to Cliff Jones, for many years Chief Examiner for CSE and GCSE government and politics, and now Chair of Examiners for this subject area, and to Dennis Harrigan, Principal Moderator and valued colleague. And, not least, this book is dedicated to all those students and examination candidates who choose to struggle with the analysis of our political system.

Colin Pilkington

INTRODUCTION

What is Politics?

Very few human beings live their lives entirely on their own: they need to live alongside other people for support and protection - in **groups, communities** and **societies**. However, despite being social animals, humans are also selfish and greedy and, left to themselves, would fight and argue all the time. Therefore, relationships between people have to be regulated and organised to prevent disagreement and conflict. In other words, each group, community or society has to have a system of law and order, so that people can live peacefully with each other. That law and order is provided by a person or group of persons whom we can call a **government**.

It can be called a government if it has three basic powers:

- The power to make laws - known as the **Legislature**

- The power to propose and carry out those laws - known as the **Executive**

- The power to enforce those laws and punish any law breakers - the **Judiciary**

These three governmental powers vary a great deal but they exist for the ruling body of any group, whether we are talking

1

about the fixtures committee of the Red Lion Darts Team or the government of the United Kingdom.

> <u>It is the study of the three powers of government, and the connections between them, that we can call politics.</u>

The word 'politics' comes from the Greek word *'polis'*, which in Ancient Greece simply meant 'a city' but, of course, in Ancient Greece a city like Athens was also a state within which people led organised lives.

> <u>Politics is the art of organising and governing a group or large collection of people.</u>

People decide on where a society is going

- they decide what its aims should be

- and they determine the way in which those aims can be realised.

- These aims and objectives for society are known as **political goals**

- Any decisions taken on how to achieve those goals are known as **policies**.

People may disagree with the aims of a society; or they may agree about the aims but disagree about the means of achieving those aims. People who roughly agree with the same aims and means will co-operate to promote those particular aims and means rather than any others. Those groups of people who share common aims and beliefs in the way society should be run are called **political parties**: they will work together to take control of government in their society and in that way ensure the implementation of their aims and objectives.

<u>The study of politics is about the rival ideas of political parties.</u>

In this book we are largely dealing with the politics of government, of which there are four levels in this country:

- **National government**, including such things as the parliament in London.

- **Regional government**, in the form of devolved government such as the Scottish Parliament or Welsh Assembly.

- **Local government**, with councils in counties, boroughs and districts.

- **European government**, through British membership of the European Union.

Power and Authority

You will often hear your friends ask, "Who gave you the right to do that?" Much the same question, or series of questions is asked in politics about the individuals, committees, councils or governments who attempt to control our lives.

- *"Who gave you the right to order us about?"*

   - *"Are you going to make me do it?"*

- "What authority do you have for saying that?"

All three questions help to explain what we mean when we use the terms **power** and **authority**.

Power is the ability both to demand that people **do** something, and to say **how a thing should be done** or organised. Dictators and unpopular governments can keep themselves in power by the use of force if required, but normally <u>the power is justified by being granted through consent - which means that the people have given their agreement to what is being done.</u>

Where **power** is granted by **consent**, the term **authority** is used:

The king had the **power** to increase the tax on beer

but

After his election the prime minister had the **authority** to ask for an increase in taxation.

When an individual or committee or any other group of people can be said to have authority, the reason which justifies that authority is known as **legitimacy**. The freely elected government of a country is often known as the **legitimate government** to make clear its difference from a body that does not have the consent of the people. During the Second World War the Germans occupied many countries in Europe and set up governments which did whatever the Germans wanted them to do. But the real governments of the occupied countries often escaped overseas to Britain where they were recognised by the free world as the **legitimate governments** of their homelands.

4

There are really three ways through which the legitimacy of government might be recognised:

a) **Tradition**: where someone claims the right to power because of years, often many centuries, of historical tradition. This power can be passed down from father to son as is the case with kings or dukes, or it might be based on the word of God, as with the Pope.

b) **Charisma**: is where people follow a leader through the strength and attraction of his or her personality, which might be good, as with Jesus Christ, or it might be evil, as with Adolf Hitler.

c) **Through the people**: is where the governing body can be said to have power because it has been freely given it by the people who are being governed, usually through some form of election. When the people as a whole take part in elections for their leaders, whether it is all the people in a country, or simply all the members of a society, this is said to be a **democracy**, with its leaders elected **democratically**.

To try to understand the difference between the forms of authority, think of your own situation at home.

If your family goes on holiday, how do you decide where to go?

- Do you go where your father wants, because you always do what he says?

  - Or do you go where your mother wants, because everyone likes her?

- Or do you have a family discussion and try to agree on what everyone wants?

When you have to decide how a government gets its authority, you can get a good idea by asking three simple questions:

government of whom?

government by whom?

government for the benefit of whom?

In the case of **democracy** these questions should give the answer:

<u>Government of the people, by the people, for the people.</u>

Representatives and Delegates

Democracy began in the tiny city states of Ancient Greece like Athens, which were so small that all the adult male citizens could meet in one place to form the governing Assembly. But. as time went by, states got larger, populations were numbered in millions and, since it was impossible to hold a single assembly for <u>all</u> the citizens, the Assembly was replaced by a meeting of the people's representatives:

True Democracy had become Representative Democracy.

Under Representative Democracy voters choose other people to represent them in parliament - or on the executive committee - or wherever. These representatives must act on behalf of and in the interests of those who elected them or they will not be chosen again at the next election. Although representatives must look after the people who voted for them they are not forced to act as the people they represent might sometimes wish them to do - MPs for example are

- free to vote as they like

  - free to speak as they like

    - free to join whichever party they like.

<u>Representative Democracy has several drawbacks:</u>

1) <u>It is not very democratic for the minority</u>. If decisions in a democracy are made by the votes of the majority, there are still large numbers of people who have no democratic voice <u>because they are always in a minority and have no say of their own</u>. This was the problem when Northern Ireland had its own assembly at Stormont, because almost a third of the population, the catholic minority, was always out-voted by the protestant majority.

2) **Elected Dictators!** Once a government is elected with a large majority, then the voters have no further say in what is done in their name until the next election. In this way Britain had a period of continuous Conservative government after 1979, despite the fact that, even in their most successful elections, the Conservatives had the support of only about 40% of the electorate. <u>Two thirds</u> of the British electorate did not vote for the party forming the government but they still had to accept what the government did.

Some assemblies, like the Labour Party Conference, are not attended by **representatives** but by **delegates**. The difference is:

- **representatives** <u>make up their own minds as to how they will vote and act and can do what their consciences tell them to do</u>.

- **delegates** <u>are given instructions as to how they will vote and act</u>.

Someone who attends the Labour Conference as a delegate for a constituency will have been told how to vote on all the proposals coming up at the conference.There would have been a meeting of the constituency party to draw up instructions for the constituency delegation and the delegates would have to follow instructions, even if they would rather vote differently themselves. This instruction as to how delegates should vote and act is called **the mandate**.

The **mandate**, as applied to politics, is based on the belief that an individual or party running for office will outline their policy in an election **manifesto**. The idea was the invention of the 19th century politician Sir Robert Peel who campaigned for election at Tamworth in 1834 when he summed up what the new Conservative Party stood for in what is now known as **the Tamworth Manifesto**. If a person or party who has presented a manifesto to the public is then elected by the public, then they are said to be <u>mandated</u> to carry out the policies contained in their <u>manifesto</u>, it is like being given a licence to do what they want to do.

For a party to be **'Mandated'** can mean two different things:

- the winners of an election **are obliged to do** what they said they would do in their manifesto and would be letting down the electors if they ratted on their promises.

- the winners of an election **have been given the right to do** what they said they would do in their manifesto. For example, if the House of Lords voted against a bill that had been passed by the House of Commons, the Lords' vote could be ignored because the Commons has a mandate <u>as an elected body</u>, while the Lords <u>are not elected</u> and do not have a mandate.

If anyone should challenge a government's right to do something, they will reply that they were given that right by putting forward their ideas in a manifesto at the time of the general election. By voting for the manifesto promises of a party the electorate have mandated that party to do as it promised. There are those who argue, however, that when it is an important matter affecting the **constitution** of the country - something like joining a single European currency or granting Scotland its own parliament - then the people should be allowed to have a say. In other words, <u>there should be a form of direct democracy instead of the representative democracy we have at the moment</u>.

The people can have their say through a **referendum**, which involves people voting, like they do in an election. But, instead of choosing between people in order to elect an MP, the voters are voting 'yes' or 'no' in answer to a political question.

- There has only ever been one national referendum in Britain and that was in 1975 when British voters voted as to whether or not the United Kingdom should remain part of the European Community.

9

- In 1979 the people of Scotland and Wales voted on whether they wanted devolution, with their own assemblies. This was repeated in 1997 when Scotland and Wales again voted on the question of devolution, as did the people of Northern Ireland on the acceptance of the Good Friday Agreement.

- In 1997 there was a referendum in London as to whether the capital should have an elected mayor.

In the past the government has always insisted that <u>a parliamentary representative democracy like Britain does not need to keep testing public opinion</u>. But this is changing and, apart from the referendums listed above, the government has promised to hold at least two more referendums:

a) Before joining <u>European Monetary Union</u> and the single currency.

b) On whether to change the voting system for Westminster elections to some form of <u>proportional representation</u>.

There are those who believe that modern developments like <u>interactive digital television</u> and the <u>Internet</u> mean that the future may include **direct democracy** with people voting on a whole range of issues by way of their television screen and computer keyboard.

The Constitution

All these ideas on <u>authority, legitimacy, the powers of government and the ordering of society</u> are brought together in the **Constitution**. Any organised body from a sporting club to the united nations has a constitution because

10 a Constitution is...

the collection of rules that:

1...defines and limits the powers of those holding offices in the organisation

2...regulates who shall hold office and how they are chosen, dismissed or replaced

3...guarantees the rights of members of the organisation

4...regulates the relations between bodies within the organisation and their relationship with ordinary members.

In most societies and in many countries like the United States of America the constitution is written out in every detail to form a document which can be referred to if any constitutional problem should arise and which can only be changed with the permission of parliament. This is known as **a written constitution**. In Britain, however, although constitutional laws are often written down they are not collected together into one document, so Britain is said to have **an unwritten constitution**.

There are four separate strands making up the British constitution:

- **The royal prerogative,** which is made up of things that the monarch can do <u>without the permission of parliament</u>. It includes calling and dissolving parliament, appointing ministers and declaring war. <u>These days the royal prerogative is in the hands of the prime minister.</u>

- **Statute law** - these are <u>constitutional laws passed by parliament</u>. An example is the law which limits the life of a parliament to five years.

- **Common law** - these are <u>decisions or rulings made by judges in court</u> which are later taken as binding on all other judges. An example was the man who went to court to claim equal rights with women, so as to get free prescriptions at the age of 60 instead of 65. Because the judge found in his favour the government has had to allow free prescriptions for all men over 60.

- **Convention** - these are ways of doing things that are not written down and not legally binding but which are done in a certain way because <u>traditionally that is how they have always been done</u>. An example is the way that the leader of the party which wins a general election is chosen to be prime minister.

For many years there have been arguments about whether we should have a written constitution or not:

Those who argue for a written constitution say that the people need a written constitution <u>to know exactly what their rights are</u>. There is a feeling that <u>governments can use the royal prerogative or conventions</u> **to avoid being answerable** <u>to parliament</u>.

hose who argue that we should keep our unwritten constitution say that <u>a written constitution is too rigid</u> and cannot be changed very easily. In America there are some strange rules about electing the President because the rules were written down two hundred years ago when it could take weeks for election results to reach Washington from distant states. A country with a written constitution cannot change with the times as is possible for those without a written constitution.

Revision Exercise 1

A good starting point for a study of politics is to ask yourself, or discuss within a group, what sort of constitution do we want and what rights should it include for us as citizens?

PART ONE

POLITICS
AND THE INDIVIDUAL

CHAPTER ONE

Political Participation

It must be remembered that, although much of this book may concentrate on the national government in Westminster - in which only a few people are involved, compared to the number of people in the country - yet the part we can all of us play in politics as individuals is every bit as important as what our MPs are doing. Margaret Thatcher, when she was prime minister, used to say that a prime minister running a country was rather like a housewife running the family home. That is something of a simplified picture but it reminds us that the decisions a family takes in day-to-day living can be said to be political. We may not think of ourselves as politicians but each one of us can be said to be involved in some sort of political activity, at some time in our lives, in one or more of the groups we belong to:

- whether it is our school or college,

- or where we work,

- or the clubs and societies to which we belong,

- or the local housing estate, village or community in which we live.

Anyone can become involved in active politics through membership of a **trade union**, **pressure group** or **political party**. Anyone can also take an interest in politics through the

media - through reading the newspapers, listening to radio news, watching television or surfing the Internet. Even if we ourselves do not wish to become a councillor or an MP, or even a party member, every one of us over the age of 18 has the right to **vote** in **elections**.

Committees

The word **committee** is defined by the dictionary as:

> a small group chosen from a larger body to make decisions about the running of that body, or to investigate some special matter concerning that body.

As such, the decision-making body of any organisation or group - from the smallest society, with a dozen or so members, to the government in Whitehall - will take the form of a committee. Therefore one can say that a committee is the basic building block of politics. Anyone is likely to be asked to serve on a committee at some time in their life and they are quite likely to be asked to act as an officer on that committee. If they do so they are very much involved in politics and the position they are holding is a political position.

The Chair of the Committee:

The position of what used to be called the **Chairman** (or **Chairwoman** if female) is very important, because the Chair functions as the leader of a committee - guiding debates, calling on members to speak, controlling and refereeing disputes, disciplining unruly members and often summing up the debate before putting it to a vote. Members of the committee speak to and through the Chair rather than address one another directly. In some committees (e.g. the Cabinet) there is no vote at the end of a discussion but the Chair (the prime minister in the case of the cabinet) will sum up what has been said and declare that to be the will of the meeting.

The Secretary

The Secretary is the most important member of a committee after the Chair. He or she sends out notices of meetings, will fix what is to be discussed and the order in which it will be discussed (the **Agenda**) in consultation with the Chair. And he or she will keep a record of what was said by the committee in the **Minutes**. In smaller societies the secretary will be appointed from among committee members but in larger organisations the secretary's duties will be carried out by a professional, as with the officials and **civil servants** who act as the **secretariat** in local and national government.

Debate

Discussions in committee are formal, with all remarks passed through the Chair, and no interruptions allowed except for **points of order** (when the speaker has got a matter of procedure wrong) or **points of information** (when the speaker has given confused, incomplete or faulty information and needs to be corrected). Discussion is limited to the items listed in advance on the Agenda, although there is usually time set aside at the end for **Any Other Business**. If a discussion goes to a vote, there has to be a required number of members present (a **quorum**); the proposal (**the motion**) requires a

proposer and **seconder** and, if there should be a tie, the Chair has the deciding or **casting** vote.

Accountability

In most cases any decisions made by a committee are **executive decisions** and need to be approved by the larger body from which the committee is drawn. In other words, anyone who acts as a representative for other people or who undertakes to carry out the duties of an office-holder, must account for their actions to the people they represent or who selected them for office. For example -

- In a society, suggestions made by the committee would be referred to the **Annual General Meeting** of the society, or to an **Extraordinary General Meeting** if it is urgent.

- In business, decisions made by a **Board of Directors** need approval by a general meeting of shareholders.

- In local government, actions of the **Education Committee** or **Housing Committee** will be endorsed by occasional meetings of the whole council.

- In national government, decisions of the **Cabinet** or **government ministers** must be approved by both houses of parliament, representing the people.

Committee members are chosen, elected or volunteer as representatives of the wider membership and therefore speak, vote and act on behalf of those they represent. Sometimes people who are not representatives are **co-opted** onto a committee for the benefit of their expert advice. These **co-**

opted members can speak in the discussions but they are not allowed to vote.

Pressure and Interest Groups

A pressure group is said to be <u>an organised group of people which seeks to influence policy, decisions and opinions.</u> In most cases the government is the body it is intended to influence but that need not be the case. There is a huge number of such groups and it is estimated that half the population belong to one or other of them. It is an important way in which people can participate in political action.

Defensive, Economic, Protection or Interest Groups:

These are not really pressure groups but they have many things in common with pressure groups. Their main purpose is to protect the interests of their own members across a wide range of issues. Typical examples are **Trade Unions**, **Professional Associations** such as the BMA or the Law Society, **Business Associations** such as the CBI or the Institute of Directors, and **Sectional Interests** such as the AA or RAC who look after motorists' interests.

These groups are distinguished by several factors -

- They work in the interests of their members and people become members of these groups out of their own self-interest.

- They are largely paid for by members' subscriptions.

- They often have many other functions beyond putting pressure on government. For example, the AA might campaign to pressurise the government over matters of interest to motorists such as roads and the cost of petrol but they also deal with members' breakdowns, publish road-maps etc.

- They often have the benefit of close contacts with government and may even be consulted by government in the framing of legislation relating to their particular field.

Sectional, Promotional or Cause Groups:

These are true pressure groups because they bring pressure to bear on behalf of those who have no influence themselves. In this instance the members of the group do not themselves benefit from the work of the group. They are paid for by donations, collections and commercial sales, while some have charity status. They are sub-divided into -

i) **Sectional** or **Promotional groups** - which exist to defend and promote groups that cannot defend and promote themselves. Into this category come groups such as **Help the Aged, RSPCA, Save the Whale, Child Poverty Action Group** and so on.

ii) **Single Issue groups** - groups that are set up for one specific purpose. They can be very small and local, as with a group of parents campaigning for a controlled crossing across a busy main road, or it can be very large and vocal as with the groups trying to prevent the building of motorways. Where other pressure groups continue year after year, single-issue groups are relatively short-lived. They are formed for one specific purpose and go out of existence when their aim has either been achieved or it becomes obvious that it never will be achieved.

iii) **Attitude groups** - which wish to change public attitudes in some way. They may wish to stop people smoking **(ASH)**, ban nuclear weapons **(CND)** or reform the electoral and political system **(Charter 88)**. The most prominent of such groups in recent years have been those dealing with conservation and allied subjects such as **Green Peace** and **Friends of the Earth**. These groups have a dual aim in that they are as interested in changing the attitudes of people in general as in bringing pressure to bear on government.

It has to be said that there is often very little distinction between these categories. CND is an issue group as much as an attitude group; Save the Whales could fit all three categories.

How Pressure Groups work

a) **Through Parliament** - Most pressure groups have MPs friendly to their interests in parliament. For some MPs this is because of their own situation, as was the case with Lord (Jack) Ashley, a former MP who is profoundly deaf, and who therefore worked tirelessly in parliament for those groups campaigning on behalf of the disabled. For other MPs it is more a career decision and they are paid a retainer by pressure groups to act on their behalf. An MP can question ministers, influence discussion in committees and so on. It

23

may be possible to introduce a Private Member's Bill: it is said that an MP winning the right to introduce a bill in the annual ballot can eat for free for some weeks as various pressure groups wine and dine the MP in hopes of getting him or her to use the bill for their cause. In recent years a number of lobbyist groups have grown up as a branch of public relations. These companies can be hired by industrial and commercial organisations to represent their interests in parliament. Sometimes, however, people like Neil Hamilton, MP for Tatton until 1997, abuse their position and act more in the interest of various lobby groups than in the interest of their constituents.

b) **Through Government and Civil Service** - There are a few important interest groups, known as **insider groups**, who have easy access to ministers and civil servants. There are also quite a number of groups who are regularly consulted during the drafting stages of a parliamentary bill or White Paper. Financial support given to the Conservative Party by the CBI and other business organisations and to the Labour Party by the Trade Unions helps to give them this 'insider' position.

c) **Through Public Opinion** - Pressure groups adopt publicity-seeking methods to get their views talked about, hoping to influence public opinion through various methods:

marches

demonstrations

public meetings

leaflets

advertisements in the press

education packs

radio and tv broadcasts

All these and more are used to catch the public's attention
and get the group's name and ideas into the mass media.
The belief is that, if you can influence public opinion, you
can influence government, because political parties have to
listen to public opinion if they want to be elected. It is not
always just the government that these methods are aimed
at: for example, conservation groups have been so successful
with public opinion among consumers that manufacturers
have found it worth their while to introduce environment-
friendly products such as unleaded petrol and re-cycled
paper.

d) **Direct Action** - Some groups, after the failure of ordinary
means, have used more extreme means of making their
views felt. Such methods can include:

strikes by Trade Unions

withholding poll tax payments

blockading ports to prevent animal exports

camping in trees to stop motorway construction

**And, of course, there is terrorism by groups like the
IRA.**

If these methods have the support of public opinion they can
be successful in changing policy - as with the poll tax

that the public does not like violence, and behaving in a way which means people getting hurt or property damaged can put the public off and turn public opinion against the protesters.

e) **In by-elections** - The most powerful weapon in the hands of pressure groups is to <u>threaten government MPs that they might lose their seats in parliament</u>. If public opinion brings pressure to bear on MPs through their local constituency parties, so that they come to believe that their constituents would vote against them, then MPs will pass on that worry to government whips. If sufficient numbers are involved, the government may well change policy. This can be seen very clearly in by-elections. Possibly the most famous example in recent years took place in 1991 when the Ribble Valley by-election was fought on the issue of the highly unpopular Poll Tax. When the Liberal Democrats won the formerly safe Conservative seat by a large majority, it was taken to be a vote against the Poll Tax. Within a few months, the tax had been abolished and the Council Tax introduced.

f) **Through Public Enquiries** - When some controversial scheme is proposed the organisation proposing the scheme may open up the proposals to public scrutiny by offering - or being forced to offer - a public enquiry. Under the control of a prominent figure such as a judge, a public enquiry will hear evidence from experts and members of the public alike. These witnesses can be questioned and challenged like witnesses in a court of law. Hearings of the enquiry are open to the general public and the results or findings of the enquiry are published for general information.

- At a local level, a public enquiry is often used as part of the planning procedure when developments like a new road or shopping centre are being built; the plans are exhibited in a public place like the library, or published in the local newspapers, or circulars are mailed to all homes in the area. The public is free to make its views known and to attempt to influence the verdict of the enquiry.

- Sometimes an enquiry which starts as a local matter achieves national importance, with major pressure and interest groups becoming involved. An example of this was the 'Sizewell B Enquiry' which examined the question of building a new nuclear reactor on the Suffolk coast. The government was in favour of the reactor but it was opposed by various environmental and anti-nuclear groups, leading to a long, complicated, bitter and well-publicised enquiry.

- A public enquiry can also be held to investigate some important event; not only to find out what happened but to make recommendations on action that should be taken as a result. An example of this was the Cullen enquiry into the shootings at the Dunblane primary school. The enquiry set out not only to understand what had happened and why the killer, Hamilton, did what he did, but also to make any recommendations that might be needed for the control of gun ownership and the rules for granting a firearms certificate.

g) **Through Europe** - In recent years pressure groups have found it very useful to work through Europe because the

European Commission actually welcomes information from pressure groups and there are established procedures which allow pressure groups to get to see influential people in the Commission and other EU bodies. <u>In Europe all pressure groups can be insider groups</u>.

Political Parties

A political party is an organisation which has policies which it wants to put into practice by <u>gaining political power</u> in central or local government. Parties are an important element in the political system since they enable voters to make sensible choices in elections, by making it clear what the candidates stand for and what sort of government or ruling group they would form.

When people vote <u>they usually vote for the party and not the individual candidate</u>

By voting as they do, <u>the people say which party they prefer in government.</u>

People can participate in politics through a party at various levels and with greater or lesser degrees of commitment:

- **Supporters:** The lowest level of support involves little more than always voting for the same party and following its fortunes in the same way as football supporters follow their favourite teams.

- **Party members:** Many members do not do much more for the party than pay their annual subscriptions, giving their financial support to the party, but they may also give up some of their time by attending some meetings or rallies and may give some practical help like putting up posters at election time, or using their cars to ferry voters to the polling stations.

- **Activist party members:** Members who are really involved in the work of the party - they will raise funds, sit on committees of the local constituency party, attend party conferences, **canvass** for votes at all election times (local as well as national) and provide a lot of simple services like addressing envelopes and providing transport on polling day.

- **Party workers:** Those who actually work for their party - as secretaries, organisers, agents, writers and advisers etc., whether in party headquarters, constituency offices or on the private staff of MPs and ministers.

- **Candidates and representatives:** Those willing to stand for office in parliament or council. There are always some dedicated people who are willing to stand so that the party is represented, even though they stand no chance of being elected.

Political parties are made up of:

The Parliamentary Party - all representatives of the party who are members of parliament (Commons or Lords). Since they are involved in the parliamentary process they are very influential because they have a say in drawing up the **party manifesto** at election time. The leader of the parliamentary party is always the leader of the party as a whole. Although the parliamentary parties have the highest profiles it must not be forgotten that there are also party organisations in the European Parliament, the Scottish Parliament, the Welsh and Northern Ireland Assemblies and in local authorities throughout the United Kingdom.

The Party in the country - this is the grass roots membership who work for and support the party, often without any wish to serve in parliament. They are usually organised into constituency parties.

Specialist groups - these can represent **sectional interests**, like groups for women or students, often as sub-divisions of constituency parties. The most prominent specialist group is formed by **the trade unions** which have an important part to play in the Labour Party.

The party leadership - is chosen in a variety of ways. The actual leader has been elected in all parties since 1965 when a Conservative leader (Edward Heath) was elected rather than chosen for the very first time.

- The leader of the <u>Conservative Party</u> in parliament is elected by the parliamentary party and is later accepted by the rest of the party. Cabinet members, shadow cabinet members and front bench spokespersons are picked by the leader.

- The leader of the <u>Labour Party</u> both inside and outside parliament is elected by <u>an electoral college</u> made up of the parliamentary party, the constituency parties and trades unions. The Shadow Cabinet when Labour is in opposition is elected at the Party Conference but a Labour prime minister is allowed to choose his or her own front bench team.

- The other parties, such as the <u>Liberal Democrats</u>, allow their general membership to have a say in the election of their leaders but not in such a wide and formalised sense as Labour.

<u>All these parts come together at the **annual party conferences** which are held every autumn, usually in seaside resorts like Blackpool or Brighton.</u>

Major parties such as the **Conservatives**, **Labour** and the **Liberal Democrats** all aspire to government (local or national) and therefore have a full range of policies for the country as a whole, in line with the general policy position of the party, which in turn is based on the underlying ideology of the party.

The nationalist parties (**SNP** in Scotland and **Plaid Cymru** in Wales) are almost totally concerned with gaining independence for their respective countries. In that respect they are a little like single-issue pressure groups, as is the **Green Party** which considers all policies from an environmental viewpoint.

In Northern Ireland the situation is different in that most parties reflect the religious divide; the **Ulster Unionists** and **Democratic Unionists** being protestant and in favour of union with Britain, the **SDLP** and **Sinn Fein** being catholic and for union with the Republic of Ireland. The **Alliance Party** of Northern Ireland is non-sectarian and liberal in its views. Northern Ireland is also unusual in having tacit support from sections of the community for political groupings that have been ready to use violent and non-parliamentary methods to achieve their political goals.

Paid and Unpaid

The British political system is very traditional and based on the way things were done in the past. One tradition underlying the British way of life is a preference for amateurs. Whether it is playing cricket or riding horses or taking part in politics, there is a suggestion that <u>someone who does something for nothing, out of love or a sense of duty, is somehow better than someone who does something in return for money.</u>

Members of Parliament

Until 1911 MPs were not paid but went into politics **"out of a sense of duty in order to serve society"**. This meant that MPs had either to be very wealthy themselves, or sponsored by a wealthy patron, or to have a profession that they could combine with being an MP. The parliamentary day which starts at two thirty in the afternoon was meant to allow MPs to follow their career as lawyers, doctors or whatever in the morning. That had to end when increasing numbers of Labour MPs were elected to parliament who did not have this financial independence. By 1999 MPs were paid just over £45,000 a year, with an expense allowance of about £49,000.

In the unreformed House of Lords members were paid an attendance allowance for days when they turned up but they got no regular salary. The Lords have been like so much else in British political life by being basically amateurs, which is why the first step on the road to reform was to declare which members of the Lords were to be regarded as **"working peers"**.

Councillors:

Councillors in local government are unpaid, although they do get expenses for travelling costs or other money laid out on council business, together with an attendance allowance to compensate them for time missed from work. Critics make two points as to why it is a mistake not to pay councillors: they are very much the arguments used in 1911 to justify paying MPs.

i) People of real ability will not stand for election because they would lose too much money if they were elected.

ii) Unpaid councillors are open to the temptation that they might be corrupted to accept money for doing *"favours"* for people who want something from the council.

Magistrates:

Although magistrates in the busy courts of the big cities are professional lawyers called **stipendiaries** (because they are paid a **stipend** *or salary*) most magistrates outside the cities are **lay magistrates** known as **Justices of the Peace** who are not trained lawyers, although they get some basic training. They serve on a part-time basis and are not paid a salary and are therefore mostly people respected locally, who have time to spare, like professional men and women, retired people, the self-employed and housewives. In court they sit as a **'bench'** of two to seven members, advised on law by a **clerk** who is legally-qualified.

Juries:

In Britain an individual has the right in serious cases <u>to be tried by his or her equals.</u> People trust ordinary citizens to be fairer to them than an over-clever judge or lawyer. **Trial by jury** is therefore one of the oldest rights in the British system (more than 700 years old). Anyone between the ages of 18 and 65 is liable to be called for jury service which is compulsory if you are called, although requests to be excused for a good reason will be considered. Jury service is not paid, although travel expenses are given, together with compensation for lost wages or salary. There is always a risk that jurors may be bribed.

Voluntary organisations:

There is a whole range of more or less political activities, from running the **Citizen's Advice Bureau** to **Prison Visitors**, which are staffed and organised by unpaid volunteers. Some of these bodies are charitable organisations and others have a great deal in common with pressure groups but they all compete for public attention and support and represent a means of serving the community. In that respect they are another way in which any individual can become involved in political action.

Revision Exercise 2:

At this point you might find it rewarding to think about the number of ways in which you yourself are involved in political activities, according to the definitions of political actions given in this chapter.

CHAPTER TWO

Opinion Formers

The Media

The term 'The Media' really stands for 'the mass media of communication' and means the ways in which information is communicated to large numbers of people. Broadly speaking, the media concerned with politics fall into three groups:

- The printed media: newspapers, magazines, leaflets and brochures, posters.

- The broadcast media: radio, television and some video or audio recordings.

- Electronic media: the Internet and inter-active tv via multimedia computers.

At the moment the last of these is still developing but potentially it is very important indeed.

The media are immensely important and influential in politics:

- For most people their information about politics is gained entirely through the media, particularly since the proceedings in parliament have been broadcast on radio

35

and television. The political information communicated by the media, and the way in which it is communicated, is of the greatest importance in influencing political opinion.

- Much of the press is **partisan** in its attitude and helps mould the public's political opinions. There is evidence that <u>the influence of the tabloid press in particular was responsible for the Conservatives' unexpected success in the 1992 general election.</u>

- Since 1959 general election campaigns have been largely fought on television. The television campaign has largely replaced public meetings and live speeches as the main way in which elections are fought. Politicians' speeches are now written with particular sentences highlighted as **'sound-bites'**, meaning those parts of the speech that will look best as 30-second excerpts in the television news.

- The first task of a pressure group trying to influence public opinion is to get its message across to the media. Many demonstrations such as marches and sit-ins do not affect the situation in themselves but, by being reported in the press and on television they manage to get the message across to the people.

The Press

The most important segment of the printed media is represented by newspapers which are sub-divided according to-

<u>their area of distribution</u>   - national, regional or local.

| their frequency | - daily, Sunday or weekly. |
| their size and format | - broadsheet or tabloid. |

Most important politically are national dailies or Sundays.

- The broadsheet newspapers of record such as the *Times, Sunday Times, Guardian, Observer, Daily* and *Sunday Telegraph, Independent* and *Independent on Sunday* are important in the way they report and reflect serious political debate by politicians and political commentators, their views sometimes having direct impact on politicians in parliament and the government.

- The tabloids such as the *Sun, Star, Daily* and *Sunday Mirror, News of the World* and *People* are far more sensational and do not treat politics very seriously. But they have a lot of influence with the mass of the people and have created some concern in the past because of the bias shown towards the Conservatives for most of the time by the majority of the tabloid press. Many people believed that a temporary shift of support towards Tony Blair by tabloid newspapers such as the *Sun* and *Daily Mail* was a major factor in helping Labour to win in 1997.

Radio and Television

The broadcast media are supposed to be free of bias, except during designated party political broadcasts. The BBC has the need to show **political balance** written into its Charter and the ITC which controls ITV and Channel 4 is also obliged to enforce **political impartiality**. Yet, despite these precautions, the BBC, Channel 4 and some ITV companies are <u>regularly accused of bias by politicians of all parties</u>. All political parties train their members to handle the media and there is often competition by politicians to appear on programmes they think are influential like Question Time on BBC1 or the Today programme on Radio Four.

Opinion Polls

Market research organisations are always testing public opinion, measuring not only party support but also the public's attitudes to party policy, party issues and the party leaders. The main customers of the polling organisations are the political parties themselves and many of these private polls are never made public. Regular monthly polls, however, are commissioned by the media and the results are published or broadcast.

Use of Opinion Polls

- The most serious use of opinion polls is that made by <u>the prime minister when choosing the date of a general election</u>. The PM obviously wants to pick a time when the party is likely to win and will therefore rely on the polls to show him or her when the party is in the lead and by how much.

- All the parties rely on the polls to tell them how popular or unpopular their policies are, so as to see how successful or unsuccessful their publicity and campaigns are proving to be.

- For the public, some people follow the fortunes of the political parties in the same way as they follow their favourite football team and rely on the opinion polls to show them the form being shown by *"their side"*.

- The opinion polls are also <u>useful to the tactical voter</u> so that, for example, an anti-government voter can look at the opinion polls to see which of the other parties is most likely to beat the government party.

- Parties are worried that <u>the polls encourage abstention</u>. If a party is shown to have a very large lead in the polls its supporters might not bother to turn out *"because they'll win anyway"* or its opponents may not vote because *"what's the point?"*

Opinion polls are not always very accurate and there have been some very bad examples of the polls getting it quite wrong on the day of the election; most notably in 1970 and 1992.

<u>There are two main reasons why the polls can and do get it wrong:</u>

- **Faulty Sampling:** Most opinion polls work with a representative sample of about 1000 people to represent the whole electorate. Each person questioned therefore represents 40,000+ voters. This is why opinion poll companies always say that there is a 3% margin of error, because one incorrect answer in the sample is multiplied many times in the results. The form of taking a sample used in the opinion polls is known as quota sampling, whereby the sample is divided into things like age, class, sex and where people live, in the same proportions as in the population as a whole, until the sample represents a

39

miniature cross-section of the population. Quite small changes in those proportions can make the whole sample inaccurate.

- **What people say they intend to do is not what they might do in reality:** Opinion polls ask the public what their future voting intentions might be. There is a strong possibility that many of those who had every intention of voting a certain way when they were questioned, might have second thoughts when polling day arrives. *For example:* In 1992 it was commonly thought that Labour were the caring party over things like health, education and unemployment, while the Conservatives were the party of self-interest and low taxes. People being questioned by an opinion poll might well have claimed that they intended to vote Labour because of they wanted the interviewer to think of them as caring persons but, when it actually came to voting in secret, the interests of self and family seemed to be more important than the appearance of caring.

Revision Exercise 3:

It is possible to examine the question of bias in the newspapers by carrying out what is called a 'media audit'. Get hold of a number of newspapers for the same day - choose a good variety - tabloid and broadsheet - and check how each of them treats the same story. How important do they think it is? How far do they sensationalise the story? Are the stories showing an obvious political party bias?

CHAPTER THREE

Voting and elections

Even if we ourselves do not wish to become a councillor or an MP, or even a party member, every one of us over the age of 18 has the right to vote in **elections**. But there are many different kinds of elections:

• <u>Local elections:</u>

Somewhere in the country there are local council elections of one kind or another every year because there are several different kinds of councils:

i) There are **District** or **Borough** Councils, which are for an area about the same size as one or two parliamentary constituencies.

ii) There are **County** Councils responsible for a whole county or shire.

iii) In certain rural areas there are **parish council** elections, but these are very small and do not really have any power except for certain duties on behalf of the community.

Councillors are elected for four years. Sometimes the whole council may stand down and be elected at one and the same time: this happens every four years. Elsewhere, elections can be spread out over three years with one third of the council retiring and being elected in each of those three years.

• <u>European elections:</u>

The United Kingdom elects 87 MEPs to the European Parliament, with elections every five years: the last election was in June 1999 which was the first British election to use proportional representation. European constituencies are very large and in Great Britain the country was divided into eleven regions each of which returned different numbers of MEPs according to the <u>regional list system</u>. In Northern Ireland three Members of the European Parliament are elected by the same <u>single transferable vote</u> form of <u>proportional representation</u> as is found in the rest of Ireland.

• <u>Parliamentary or Westminster General Elections:</u>

These concern the 659 constituencies electing representatives to the House of Commons. The date of a general election is chosen by the prime minister if the government is not dismissed by a vote of no confidence. According to the law a general election must take place <u>within five years</u> of the previous general election.

• <u>By-elections:</u>

A by-election takes place when the seat of an MP, MEP or local councillor becomes vacant through death, retirement or resignation and an election must be held to replace him or her.

<u>Note that all these elections are traditionally held on a Thursday and that local elections are always held on the first Thursday in May.</u>

Apart from the above elections, which are obviously political, there are also other kinds of elections which affect most people at one time or another, and which are known as **Organisational elections** and which usually concern the election of officers in Trade Unions, clubs and societies etc.

Voting procedure

a) When an election is called, **candidates** are **nominated** for the **ward** or **constituency**.

b) Nomination is made according to certain rules concerning:

   i) **qualifications** - qualifications are different depending on whether it is a local, European or parliamentary election.

   ii) **nomination** requirements - nomination papers have to be signed by a specified number of residents in the ward or constituency.

   iii) In parliamentary elections candidates must pay a **deposit** of £500, which they get back if they gain more than a minimum number of votes.

c) Papers for candidates have to be submitted to the **Returning Officer** for that election by a certain **Nomination Day**.

d) Candidates then **campaign** for election over a three-week period.

e) The **electorate** gains the right to vote by having their names entered on the **Electoral Register** (or **Electoral**

Roll), a new one of which is drawn up each February. The age qualification to be allowed to vote is 18, but other qualifications differ depending on whether it is a local, European or parliamentary election.

f) When an election is due, all those entitled to vote receive a **polling card**, quoting their number on the electoral register and stating where their **polling station** is situated. More often than not the polling station is a local school but any suitable building may be used such as a church hall, community centre or Scout or Guide hut.

g) On election days the polling stations are open from 8 a.m. if it is a local election, but from 7 a.m. for parliamentary elections. The polls close at 9 p.m. for local elections and at 10 p.m. for a parliamentary election.

h) On the day of the election the elector has his or her name checked against the register on arrival at the polling station and is issued with a **ballot-paper** listing the candidates. The voter takes the ballot paper into a <u>screened booth</u> and marks a pencilled cross against the name of the preferred candidate (<u>any other mark makes it a</u> **spoiled paper**). The paper is then folded and placed into a locked and sealed **ballot-box**. All these precautions are to make sure that it is a **Secret Ballot** and that there is no **electoral malpractice** such as the same person voting more than once.

When the polling stations close, the ballot boxes are taken to a central location where the **Count** is to take place. The votes are counted and the Returning Officer announces the result.

Electoral Systems

There is a lot of argument over the sort of electoral system we should use in this country. Some systems are proposed because they are fair, others because they give clearcut results and always provide for a winning party. But there is no clear agreement about which system is best because there are many different purposes served by holding an election and the different purposes do not always agree with one another.

The purposes of different electoral systems

There are five things to look for when choosing an electoral system.

1. <u>Reflection of public opinion</u> - An election should produce a parliament, council etc. that represents the shades of public opinion in the electorate.

2. <u>Choosing a representative</u> - Voters want someone in parliament or on the council to look after their interests, whom they can vote out of office at the next election if the member fails in these duties.

3. <u>All votes should count</u> - Only votes which go towards electing a representative have any value. Any others are wasted votes.

4. <u>Choice of government</u> - The result should make one of the parties contending the election a clear winner allowing them to form a government or take the chair in local councils, without having to make any deals.

5. <u>Voters should understand the system</u> - The mechanics of the voting system should not be hard to understand.

Majority Systems

- are electoral systems in which candidates with the most
    votes win and losers get nothing.

1. Single member-simple majority, also known as First past the post (FPTP)

From a list of candidates the voter chooses one. The candidate with more votes than any other candidate, even if it is only one vote more, wins outright. The system is

- easy to understand

    - the result can be quickly announced

        - the outcome is usually clear-cut

            - small constituencies have an easily identified member.

This system was used in Great Britain (although not in Northern Ireland) for all elections until 1999 and continues, at least at the moment, to be the system used for elections to the Westminster Parliament and for local government in England and Wales.

2. Overall majority systems

These are systems where the eventual winner is supported by over 50% of the electorate.

i) In the **Second Ballot** system, as used in France, if no one candidate gets 50% of the vote on the first ballot then all but the top two candidates are eliminated and those two put themselves forward in a second ballot a week later.

ii) In the **Alternative Vote** or **Supplementary Vote** systems the voter lists the candidates in order of preference. If any candidate gains more than 50% of first preference votes they are elected outright; if no one candidate gains more than 50%, then second preference votes are re-allocated until one candidate has gained more than 50%.

A variation on the Alternative Vote system has been recommended to the Labour Party by the Jenkins Commission as the system to be used in future Westminster elections. But it is not regarded with much favour by either of the two major parties.

Proportional Systems

- are systems which award seats to parties according to the preferences of the electorate.

3. List systems

The elector votes for a party rather than an individual and seats in the elected body are assigned to parties in proportion to the percentage of votes cast for each party. The parties prepare lists of candidates and seats are allocated to names on these lists. If a party won 10% of the votes to a 100-seat assembly, the top ten names on the party list would be given seats. A regional list system was used for the European Parliament elections in Britain for the first time in 1999. Scotland and Wales were single regions electing 8 and 5 MEPs respectively. England was divided into the nine regions of North East (4), North West (10), Yorkshire and the Humber (7),

West Midlands (8), East Midlands (6), Eastern (8), South West (7), South East (11) and London (10).

4. Single Transferable Vote (STV)

A system devised in Britain to produce constituency members in a proportional system and used for all elections in the Republic of Ireland, as well as European and local elections in Northern Ireland. It involves large multi-member constituencies, each constituency electing up to five members. For example, in the European elections the whole of Northern Ireland votes as one constituency and elects three MEPs. A successful candidate has to achieve a quota of votes arrived at by dividing the votes cast by the number of seats available. Second and other preferences come into play partly by re-distributing votes from candidates gaining least first preference votes and also from re-assigning votes surplus to the quota for successful candidates. It is very complicated but is very fair and ensures that no votes are wasted. It is the system promoted by the Electoral Reform Society and is the voting system advocated by the Liberal Democrats.

5. Additional Member (AMS)

A system which attempts to combine proportional and majority systems in a mixture of Simple Majority and List systems. The elector votes twice, once for a candidate and once for a party. Some seats in parliament are filled by constituency MPs elected by a simple majority, others are filled from party lists. If a party wins 40% of the vote but only 25% of the constituency seats they are given enough places from the list as to make up their share of parliamentary seats to 40%. Variations of this system were introduced for the elections to the Scottish Parliament and Welsh Assembly. In Scotland a parliament of 129 seats is divided between 73 normal constituency seats and 56 regional top-up seats. In Wales a 60-seat Assembly is divided between 40 constituency seats and 20 regional top-ups. An example of how the system operates can be seen in how it affected the Conservatives in Scotland. Although they actually did not win a single first-past-the-post constituency they were given eighteen regional seats to become the third largest party in the Scottish Parliament.

Political Socialisation

How do people learn their political attitudes? Many people believe that individuals learn their political beliefs as they grow up - from their family, from their friends and the people around them and from their environment. This theory says that there are all sorts of things in our lives and our upbringing that help us decide how we will vote and which political party we shall support. These sort of things include:

Our Parents: Large numbers of people vote for the same party as their parents and grandparents. Sometimes parents and children do not get on with each other, and the children may deliberately vote in a different way to their parents as a protest.

Social Class: Labour is traditionally seen as the party of the Working Class and the Conservatives as the party of the Middle Class. This has changed a bit in recent years and, although working class voters who are unskilled, belong to unions and live in council houses are still strong Labour supporters, the skilled, non-unionised and home-owning working classes have been known to vote Conservative.

Area or Region: Where you live has an influence on the way you vote. <u>Inner city areas, council estates and mining areas are likely to vote Labour. Country areas and middle class suburbs are often Conservative</u>. In the country as a whole, Scotland, South Wales and Northern England are largely Labour, while Southern England is mostly Tory or Lib Dem.

Age: Young people want change and the old want things to stay the same as they have always been. This means that young people will vote for the party that offers change, whether it is Conservative or Labour or any other party. Young people are also more likely to be fed up with all political parties and to vote for no one.

Gender: It was once believed that women were more likely to support the Conservatives than men were. Opinion polls have shown that, while this is true, there is only a 2% difference in support between men and women, and that is too small a difference to mean anything.

Ethnic origins: Asian and Afro-Caribbean electors are more likely to vote Labour than they are to vote Conservative. However, since <u>ethnic minorities tend to live in inner city areas, with low-paid jobs and high rates of unemployment</u>, it might well be that it is things like that, rather than their ethnic origin, which make their minds up as to which way to vote.

Voting Behaviour

Issue-based Voting: In this form of voting the voters decide what the most important issues are as far as they or their families are concerned, and then vote for the party which they think has the best policies to deal with those issues, <u>as if choosing from a shopping list.</u>

There is a difference between what people say are the important issues and what they really think are worth voting about. Before the 1992 election the issues that people claimed were important were the National Health Service, Education and Unemployment - all Labour issues. Yet the Conservatives won. After the election Ivor Crewe wrote, "*Had electors voted solely on the main issues Labour would have won*". In fact, the issue that won the 1992 general election was the number of people who were afraid that Labour would increase taxes too much and who believed, rightly or wrongly, that only the Tories can deal with the economy.

Negative Voting: It is assumed that people vote because they want a certain party to win the election. <u>But just as often they are voting to stop a party winning</u>. It has been said that "Oppositions do not win elections - Governments lose them". In other words, <u>it is not so much a case of people voting **for** the opposition as people voting **against** the government.</u> This has led in recent years to what is called **negative campaigning**, in which political parties have campaigned not by saying what they themselves would do but by trying to make the electorate worried or scared at what the other party would do. The 1992 election was notorious for the way in which the Conservatives, backed by a Tory press, tried to frighten the electorate with what the Labour Party and its leader, Neil Kinnock, might do. "*Nightmare on Kinnock Street*", shouted headlines in the *Sun*. But all parties are guilty of negative campaigning with scare tactics and stories of scandal intended to put the electorate off voting for the others.

Tactical Voting: This involves voting so as <u>to prevent a result you do not want.</u> By tactical voting, electors vote for whichever party has the best chance of <u>beating the most unpopular party</u>. For example, if you were a Labour supporter but it was more important to get the Tory out than to get Labour in, you might very well vote Liberal Democrat if they were more likely to beat the Tories than Labour in that particular seat.

Protest Voting: Every government is unpopular and a governing party always loses support between general elections. This shows in the number of by-elections that the government party loses, because many protest voters want to warn the government. <u>They feel safe to vote against their own party when it does not affect the situation in Parliament</u>. By the time of the 1997 general election, the Conservative government had not won a single by-election since 1989.

- The protest vote is important in local elections. The voters do not vote on local issues but as a comment on politics at Westminster. Even good and efficient councils can be thrown out because of the unpopularity of their party nationally.

- Third parties do best from the protest vote. For example, in 1999 traditional Labour supporters became rather disenchanted with the Labour government. In the May devolution elections in Scotland and Wales, in local council elections and in the European elections of June, disgruntled Old Labourites expressed their dissatisfaction by switching to the Scottish Nationalists, Plaid Cymru and the Greens. Even more significantly huge numbers refused to vote at all.

Abstention: The average turnout in general elections is about 75%. The turnout in local elections is usually between 33% and 43% but in recent years has become increasingly lower. In the 1999 European elections the turnout was only 25%. <u>There are always some electors who do not vote</u>. Many of them cannot be bothered - the weather is bad or they are tired after a day's work or there is something good on television. <u>Others, however, abstain from voting for definite reasons</u>.

- It is a protest vote in that the electors wish to protest at what their party is doing but cannot bring themselves to vote for any of the other parties.

- The voter may support a party like the Green Party which does not have a candidate standing in that constituency.

- The voter may dislike all the candidates to the extent of feeling unable to vote for any one of them. This is particularly true in local elections.

There have been instances of elections being lost not because the winning candidate's vote has gone up but because so many of the defending party's supporters abstained.

Revision exercise 4:

Are you old enough to vote yet?

Do you intend to vote in the next general election?

Will you also vote in the next local elections?

If you do not intend to vote, why are you not going to vote?

Do you know what party you will support?

What made you support that party?

PART TWO

STRUCTURES & PROCESSES

CHAPTER FOUR

Parliament

The word 'parliament' comes from the French word *'parler'* (to speak) and therefore was the name given in the Middle Ages to the group of men assembled to advise the king by discussing military, judicial and financial policy. Parliament has two meanings:

1 **The Parliament** is the actual place, housed in London in the Palace of Westminster. This is a vast building with many offices and committee rooms as well as the two debating chambers, but it is too small to contain all members of parliament and many have to use offices in other buildings. Parliament is a **bi-cameral** (two-chamber) assembly with a non-elected upper house, the **House of Lords**, and an elected lower house, the **House of Commons**.

2 **A Parliament** is the assembly of people and their representatives which used to be called by the monarch when needed - usually in order to provide money. A parliament in those days would be for as long as was necessary - it might last for little more than a week and there could be several parliaments within a year. Or it could last for many years, like the Long Parliament summoned in 1640, which was only dissolved in 1660. Today, a parliament changes when there is a general election and there is a

maximum period that a parliament can last - <u>five years since 1911</u>. In theory the monarch dissolves parliament and calls a new general election but in fact the timing of both is in the hands of the prime minister. A parliament is divided up into year-long **Parliamentary Sessions**, running from November to November. Each session begins with the **State Opening of Parliament** when the monarch delivers the **Royal Speech** to both houses of parliament in a ceremonial demonstration that government in Britain is by **the Crown in Parliament**.

The Crown

Britain is what is known as a **constitutional monarchy**. Once the king was the sole ruler, with absolute powers, but after the Civil Wars between King and Parliament, the **Bill of Rights** of 1689 established that the monarch was subject to constitutional law. Since that time all remaining political powers have been taken away from the monarch so that it is now said that <u>the Queen reigns but does not rule</u>.

The rights and privileges of the monarch to do things without reference to parliament are known as the **Royal Prerogative**. Between the Bill of Rights and the nineteenth century many of these powers were taken over by parliament, but a number of what are known as **discretionary powers** remain and can be used by the government to do things without their being discussed or approved by parliament, including:

- The power to sign treaties and make war.

- The power to dissolve parliament and call an election.

- The power to appoint and dismiss government ministers.

- The power of patronage through:

  - appointment to a range of posts in Church and State such as Bishops, officers in the armed services, senior civil servants and judges.

  - the granting of honours such as peerages and knighthoods.

  - the awarding of government posts.

  - appointment to public bodies such as the BBC, NHS or a wide variety of quangos.

The royal prerogative has slowly passed out of the hands of the monarch personally and is now exercised on behalf of the monarch by the prime minister and government. The expression 'the Crown', which used to mean the monarch as wearer of the crown, is now used as a general term to mean the body of ministers which forms the government. The only remaining expression of the historic 'Crown in Parliament' is in the annual State Opening of Parliament when the monarch speaks to the assembled Lords and Commons from her throne in the House of Lords and delivers a speech outlining the intended parliamentary programme for the forthcoming session. On these occasions the Queen's Speech is delivered by the queen as if it were what she thought herself, spoken in her own words, but, in fact, it is written by the Prime Minister's office and is a policy statement by the governing party over which the queen herself has no control.

The position of the monarch in the constitution is that of head of state and not head of government. The monarch is seen as a figurehead and a symbol of national unity like the flag or national anthem. The monarch is supposed to be non-political so as to represent the nation as a whole and not just the minority that would be represented by a political party. This is claimed to be one of the strengths of having a monarchy rather than an elected president. The monarch is kept aware of political developments through weekly meetings with the prime minister but will not even make statements which could be interpreted as political, let alone become involved in political activity.

Any involvement in a political argument by the monarch would create a **constitutional crisis**. The use of the royal prerogative by the prime minister means that a monarch does not have to make political decisions since there are established **conventions** in place to take those decisions on the monarch's behalf. The one occasion when the monarch might be faced with a political choice is if, after a general election, there was no winning party with a clear majority in the House of Commons. The normal convention of sending for the leader of the largest party to become prime minister would not be possible and the identity of the prime minister, and the party which would then become the governing party, would be decided by the personal choice of the monarch - although, obviously, with a lot of advice.

The House of Commons

The House of Commons is sometimes called the **Lower House** because the House of Lords is older and, in a country as class-conscious as Britain, an assembly of the upper classes was thought of as being superior to mere commoners. The Commons, so-called because they are separate from the

Nobility or the Church and represent the ordinary people, were admitted to parliament as early as the thirteenth century, at first in order to raise taxes for the king but, over the centuries, they have increased their importance until today the House of Commons is the dominant chamber.

- The prime minister is always chosen from the Commons.

- Important debates and measures are always introduced in the Commons.

- Only the Commons has the right to vote on money bills - *in* other words, only the Commons can authorise taxation and government spending.

The source of the Commons' authority is the fact that, unlike the Lords where the members only represent themselves, members of the Commons are there as representatives of the people in their constituencies. The House of Commons is **democratic** - <u>its members are there because the people have voted for them.</u>

Each member of the House of Commons represents an average of **60,000** voters, so the size of the House varies according to the population. In 1900 there were over 700 members but this figure went down when Ireland was granted independence in 1922. In 1945 there were 630 MPs; raised to 635 in 1974; 650 in 1983; 651 in 1992 and finally to 659 members after the end of the 1992 parliament. There are more MPs than will fit comfortably into the Palace of Westminster.

In the debating chamber of the Commons, benches of seats are arranged into two blocks so as to face one another, across a gap which is wider than the length of two sword blades (this is a reminder of the days when members had to be persuaded not

61

to stab one another when the argument got heated). At the head of the chamber a **clerks' table** is placed between the two sides, on which is placed the **Mace** while the house is sitting. Beyond this sits **the Speaker** who chairs the debates, keeps order and rules on which members are allowed to speak. Members supporting the government sit on the Speaker's right, members opposed to the government sit on the Speaker's left. On both sides the rows of benches are broken by a central gangway. The **front bench** above the **gangway** on the government side (the **Treasury Bench**) is reserved for the prime minister and other members of the government. The front bench above the gangway on the opposition side is reserved for the leader and shadow cabinet members of the largest opposition party - the **Official Opposition**. Below the gangway sit the front bench representatives of the minor opposition parties such as the Liberal Democrats or nationalist parties. The majority of ordinary MPs without front bench responsibilities are known as **backbenchers**.

A full House of Commons is elected in a general election, to serve for a **term** - which is as long as the prime minister wishes, <u>but must not exceed five years</u>. A term is divided into year-long **sessions**. And a session is divided by **recesses**, or holidays, at Christmas, Easter, Whitsun and summer. The summer recess is particularly long, with members away from Westminster from July to November. In all, parliament meets for about 150 days each year. The daily timetable in the Commons varies because most MPs' time is taken up with office and constituency work and, <u>most importantly, with sitting on committees.</u> But most attention centres on the debating chamber because that is what is seen most on television.

In the debating chamber the day begins at 2.30 in the afternoon with **Question Time** - during which three or four ministers a day will answer questions from backbenchers, the various ministers taking it in turns to answer questions for about fifteen minutes each. **Prime Minister's Question Time** is unusual in being for 30 minutes on Wednesday afternoons. Question Time is followed by the day's **debate**, as stated on the MPs' timetable known as an **order paper**. Debates go on until ten in the evening when a vote, or division, may take place. Unless there is urgent business the house will end, or **rise**, at 10.30 p.m after an **adjournment debate**. On Fridays, and more recently on Wednesdays as well, the Commons sits in the morning, with **sittings** beginning at 9.30 a.m. Friday sessions are increasingly poorly attended and are largely devoted to **private members' bills**.

Media reporting of parliament concentrates on the debating chamber, as if debates were the most important part of parliamentary activity. This is not really the case. The important work - the scrutiny of legislation and the government, takes place in committees, of which there are two main types:

1. Standing committees:

Up to ten standing committees are set up for each parliamentary session, with between 25 and 50 members in each. Membership is allocated to the various parties in proportion to the representation of those parties in the House. Some standing committees consider procedural matters and others look at European legislation, but the real work of standing committees is at the **Committee Stage** of the legislative process between the Second and Third Readings,

63

when each bill is scrutinised sentence-by-sentence by one of up to eight standing committees established for this purpose; bills being taken in turn by committees labelled A - H.

2. Select committees:

These are what are called *"watchdogs with teeth"* and exist to examine government administration, expenditure and policy. They have 11 members, all backbenchers, with a government majority of one, and they are appointed for the life of a parliament. The main select committee is the **Public Accounts Committee**, over 100 years old and concerned with the raising and spending of public money. But, since 1980, there have been **departmental select committees** covering the work of all the major government departments. They work by conducting the equivalent of a judicial enquiry, including the cross-examination of witnesses and with the ability to summon individuals - even ministers - to appear before them to give evidence.

Other types of committees include -

- **Joint committees**, where members of both Lords and Commons serve together on a select committee for a particular purpose.

- Internal **Party committees** such as the Parliamentary Labour Party or the Tories' 1922 Committee.

- A **Committee of the Whole House**, which is when all 659 members of the House of Commons meet as a committee, usually to consider the committee stage of the Budget but also for constitutional matters such as the Maastricht Treaty.

Officers of the House of Commons

1. The Speaker

All parliamentary debates are chaired by the **Speaker**, or by one of three **Deputy Speakers**. But the Speaker is more than simply the chairperson in debates: he or she is <u>the embodiment of the Commons and symbol of the authority of Parliament.</u>

The Speaker is chosen from the ranks of sitting MPs by the votes of the House and is usually an experienced and knowledgeable parliamentarian who is respected by members of all parties. There is no rule about this, but in the recent past members of the Conservative and Labour parties have alternated as Speaker (*Horace King [Lab], Selwyn Lloyd [Con], George Thomas [Lab], Bernard Weatherill [Con] and Betty Boothroyd [Lab]*). The Speaker remains an MP, with constituency duties, but he or she cannot take part in debates, nor can the Speaker vote, except in the case of a tie, when the casting vote must be given to the existing situation and against change. It is expected that the Speaker will resign from his or her party on taking up office but, if there is a general election, it is a convention that the major parties do not put up candidates against the Speaker.

As chair of Commons sittings, the Speaker follows committee rules, naming those members permitted to speak, who will then address their remarks to the Speaker or Deputy Speaker. The Speaker gets to know the names of all MPs and will keep a record of who has been called on to speak and how often so as to maintain the tradition of impartiality and balance. The Speaker will also rule on the admissibility of amendments, on points of order or information and on whether requests for emergency debates should be granted. The Speaker is an expert in **Erskine May**, the rule-book which decides how the Commons should function.

The Speaker is responsible for discipline in the House, mostly confined to shouts of 'Order'. But for a more serious problem, such as disorderly behaviour, unparliamentary language or constantly ignoring the Speaker's rulings, the Speaker can "*name*" an offending MP, thereby excluding him or her from the House for five days or more. For disciplinary matters the Speaker is assisted by the **Serjeant-at-Arms** who can escort an MP from the House, by force if necessary. In the last resort there is a cell in the tower housing Big Ben, where the unruly MP can be imprisoned temporarily.

The Speaker is also head of the Commission which employs staff and provides accommodation and services for the Commons. The Speaker will also summon and chair any committee considering electoral reform or changes to parliamentary procedure and he or she also has ultimate responsibility for the ten-yearly **constituency boundary review.**

2. The Leader of the House

The Leader is a party politician and, these days, usually a member of the Cabinet. He or she is appointed to manage parliamentary affairs in the Commons for the government so as to ensure the smooth passage of government business. In association with the government **Chief Whip** and his or her Opposition shadow counterpart, the Leader of the House will determine public business for the following week, issue order papers, hear requests for emergency debates and generally ensure that the Commons is working smoothly. At least once a week, during question time, the Leader will make a statement to the House about the timetable and agenda of the next week.

3. Clerk of the House

This is the senior official of the Commons, employing 150 clerical and administrative staff. The Clerk keeps the official journal of the House and is principal adviser on practice and procedure to the Speaker, Leader and MPs in general. The Clerk is appointed internally from the Clerk's staff so that whoever holds the position has long experience of the House of Commons and its procedures.

The House of Lords

The **Second Chamber**, or **Upper House**, is the unelected part of Parliament. Directly descended from the Great Council which advised medieval kings, the House of Lords represents the First and Second Estates - the Nobility and the Church. Debates in the House of Lords, and all judicial proceedings, are chaired by **the Lord Chancellor**, who is also the nation's senior judge - responsible for the courts, the judiciary and the legal professions. To signify his importance, the Lord Chancellor sits upon the Woolsack, representing the fact that Britain's wealth was traditionally made through the wool trade.

The composition of the House of Lords (until December 1999) is:

Archbishops and bishops of the Church of England	26
Law Lords	20
Hereditary peers (who can pass on their titles)	777
Life peers (whose titles die with them)	382

It should be noted that 18 hereditary peers and 61 life peers were women.

The only other parliament in the western world to have hereditary members is that of Belgium, and that is restricted to three members of the royal family. The fact that the House of Lords is undemocratic and in need of reform has been a political issue for some time but it was left to the Labour government elected in 1997 to proceed with a realistic programme of reform. Early in 1999 a bill was presented to parliament with the aim of removing hereditary peers as from December 1999,with the aim of producing a transitional House of Lords largely made up of life peers, although a possible 91 might well remain for a transitional period. The same bill introduced measures to increase the number of Labour or Liberal Democrat life peers to achieve a better party balance over the transitional period.

The proposed composition of the reformed House of Lords is the subject of a long debate pn whether life peers should be **elected** or **nominated**. On this question the government offered four possible alternatives:

1: A fully nominated chamber, possibly based on representatives of various industries and professions, to gain a range of specialist, expert opinion.

2: A directly elected chamber based on the full electorate.

3: An indirectly elected chamber made up of representatives from the devolved assemblies, local government and European Parliament.

4: A mixture of nominated and elected members.

The problem with these options is that nomination is no more democratic than the present system, while an elected chamber would challenge and weaken the authority of the Commons. The timetable for reform assumes that the government's proposals will have gained the approval of parliament before the date of the next general election, so that plans for reform can be fully debated in the election campaign.

Whips

In fox-hunting the men who keep the pack of hounds under control are known as **'whips'** and it is from them that the MPs and peers who are responsible for party discipline in parliament get their name. Like their namesakes, the **Whips**

- keep the party together

- keep party members all moving in the same direction

- prevent troublesome individuals from going off on their own.

When an MP enters parliament as a representative of a political party, he or she is said to **'accept the party whip'** - by claiming to belong to a party the MP is accepting the discipline enforced by the party whips. If an MP rebels against the party discipline and is effectively thrown out of the party it is said that **'the party whip has been withdrawn'**.

The **Government Chief Whip** is an important figure, an automatic member of the cabinet and the only person apart from the prime minister and the chancellor to have an official residence in Downing Street (number 12). A chief whip has a number of assistant whips and appointment to the **Whips' Office** is always thought to be a good promotion for ambitious young MPs. In the Conservative Party the leader chooses the whips, but in the Labour Party they are elected by the Parliamentary Party (PLP*)*.

The Whips are like party managers. They:

- advise the party leaders about opinion among backbench MPs.

- advise the party leaders about possible rebellions and how to avoid them.

- comfort and advise MPs who have doubts about their loyalty.

- make recommendations to party leaders about possible promotions or demotions.

- keep their ears to the ground to know what MPs are saying, thinking and doing.

The most important task of the whips is in seeing that all MPs in their party vote when the House divides and, what is more, <u>make sure that MPs vote in the way that the party wants</u>. Each week the **government and opposition whips** meet with the **Leader of the House** and agree the programme and timetable for the following week. That timetable, including when divisions are likely to take place, is then printed as an order paper. Copies of these are sent to every MP in the parliamentary party by the **Whips' Office**, with all the issues calling for a division underlined to show how important it is that the MPs should vote. <u>Minor issues</u> are underlined once (**one-line whip**), <u>where an MP is expected to vote</u> it is underlined twice (**two-line whip**) and <u>where an MP's vote is essential</u> it is underlined three times **(three line whip)**.

When a government has a small majority, every vote counts and whips will do almost anything to get all their members to turn out. (In the last days of the 1974-79 Labour government there were ambulances bringing sick MPs from hospital to vote and rumours that MPs had been carried though the lobbies on stretchers.) If an MP cannot vote through absence or ill-health the whips will find an MP on the opposing side who also needs to be away and <u>they will</u> **'pair'** <u>the two MPs</u> to cancel out each others' non-votes.

In order to get a reluctant MP to vote, or prevent a rebel from abstaining or voting against their own party, the whips will plead with the MPs, promise them promotion or some perk like a better office, threaten them with the opposite, even use blackmail. Whips have even been known to make MPs cry. The ultimate punishment is **to withdraw the party whip**, like the 8 Tory rebels over Europe who were refused the whip in 1994-5.

The only occasion when the whip is not applied in voting is when the House is allowed a **'Free Vote'** when it is said that

71

the "whips are off". These take place on issues that are <u>affairs of the MP's conscience</u> rather than party policy, such as capital punishment, abortion or Sunday opening. On a free vote there is a cross-party division of personal opinions and it is no longer a matter of party discipline.

Revision exercise 5:

<u>MPs are expected to vote according to the instructions of party whips.</u>

<u>Yet, how do you think an MP should decide how to vote -</u>

<u>According to their conscience or for the good of the country?</u>

<u>In the interests of, or according to the ideas of, the MP's constituents who elected that MP to represent them?</u>

<u>In line with the instructions of the party whips to support party policy and unity?</u>

CHAPTER FIVE

The Functions of Parliament

The main functions of a parliament:

- **Legislation:** Parliament is the legislature for the United Kingdom. All proposed laws must be debated and approved by parliament before they become **statute law**.

- **Money Supply:** The raising and spending of public money can only be done with the consent of parliament. Traditionally since the fourteenth century, and by constitutional law since 1911, the House of Lords has no say over money supply, which is a matter solely for the Commons.

- **Scrutiny:** Control of the supply of money to the monarch originally gave parliament the ability to have control over the actions of the king and his government (the executive). This is still the case and all government ministers are accountable to parliament for their actions: through written or spoken questions, in debate or through their appearance before parliamentary committees.

Sovereignty

Sovereignty is said to belong to any state, body or individual which has complete control over its own affairs, without having to refer to a higher authority which must be obeyed. In Britain we are said to have **parliamentary sovereignty** because no other body in the country has the right to make and unmake laws except parliament. Even those authorities which seem to pass laws - such as local councils - can only pass **by-laws**, because they have been granted that right by parliament, within certain limits, in what is known as **delegated legislation**. There are those who argue that Britain has lost sovereignty because of membership of the **European Union** but a parliamentarian would argue that we are members of the EU because parliament voted for our membership, thus making membership our sovereign decision.

The Functions of the House of Commons

<u>In structural terms the House of Commons has three main functions:</u>

Legislation

The Commons has an important role to play in making laws. Most legislation takes the form of **public bills**, prepared and proposed by the government, but there are also **private members' bills** which are proposed laws put forward by individual MPs, with or without support. **Private bills** are laws passed to allow individuals or organisations to undertake something that is normally a state concern: private bills were needed, for example, to authorise the construction of the Severn Bridge or the Channel Tunnel. **Delegated legislation** is the granting of powers to government ministers or public bodies so that they can issue rules and regulations concerning their sphere of activity.

Scrutiny

A principal duty of the House of Commons is to scrutinise and check the workings of government. This is done in **debate**, either by speaking in government sponsored debates, or in debates initiated by the Opposition (there are 19 days each year when the Opposition can choose the subject to be debated), or an MP can ballot for the chance to propose the 30-minute **adjournment debate** which closes each day's sitting of the Commons. Most scrutiny of government takes place in committees (*see below*) but an immense amount of work goes into questions to ministers, of which some 50,000 are asked in each parliamentary session. Spoken questions and answers at **Question Time** get media attention but written questions and answers are more important because they demand more carefully considered answers.

Scrutiny is all about **accountability** which is the idea that all members of the government should account for their actions to someone. Since government ministers are supposed to be acting in the interests of the people, they should be open to questions as to what they are doing and how well they are doing it, from MPs in their role of representatives of the people.

75

Representation

An MP is in the Commons to represent a constituency and its inhabitants. An MP must therefore deal with the questions and problems of constituents and represent the interests of the area covered by that constituency in parliament.

The Duties of an MP

An MP is elected as a representative, with three areas for which he or she is responsible:

- the MP's party

    - the MP's special interests

        - the MP's constituency

1 - Party:

Parliament is organised on party lines - there is the **government party** and there are several **opposition parties**. The Opposition is the name given to all those MPs whose parties do not have a place in the government and therefore the Opposition is usually made up of more than one political party. Each individual MP has a part to play in the party battle. On behalf of his or her party an MP must:

- Vote whenever required to do so, in the debating chamber and in committee.

- Speak in debates, or act in committee, so as to support party policy.

- Belong to party committees or discussion groups, to support the party organisation in parliament.

- Obey party whips at all times, by acting as instructed in order papers issued by the whips, especially when the whips have marked an issue as being important by underlining it three times, creating a **three-line whip**.

- Support the party outside parliament - through the media, by making speeches or giving talks, through promotional or fund-raising activities (especially for the MP's constituency party), as members of all-party groups or delegations.

2 - Special Interests:

An MP can act for various special interests, either by representing them to parliament or representing parliament to them. This representation can take different forms:

- **Sponsorship** - as is often the case with Labour MPs who are sponsored by trade unions. The union helps with money for the election campaign and gives some money to the MP's constituency party. In return the MP obviously keeps an eye on the union's interests.

- **Personal interest** - an MP is influenced by his or her career or special circumstances. For example, an MP who is a farmer will look after farming interests; while a disabled MP will keep the disabled in mind.

- **Advisers and consultants** - companies, charities, pressure groups, trade associations and similar bodies will pay MPs to act as their parliamentary advisers or consultants, sometimes making the MP a director of the company.

- **Lobbyists** - MPs can also help professional public relations companies who want to gain access to parliament.

MPs must declare their interests in the **MPs' Register of Interests** and, since the **Nolan Committee** reported, they must also declare any money or gifts they receive from outside interests. It is in everyone's interests to know that when an MP argues for a certain cause or votes in a certain way, he or she does so out of public interest and not because someone is paying them to do so.

3 - Constituency:

An MP is supposed to work in the interests of the geographical area, or constituency, that he or she represents. Most MPs spend 2 - 3 days a week and many weekends on constituency matters and a good MP will try to visit the constituency as often as possible; even if it is far away from London. Constituency work can take two forms:

i) <u>Helping constituents with their problems</u>, which might be problems with a government department, the local council or a business organisation. The constituent might write to the MP, or see the MP personally by "**lobbying**" the MP in parliament, or attending the "**surgery**" an MP will hold in the constituency. The MP will take up the matter with the relevant government department until a satisfactory answer is received. Every month 15,000 letters are written to ministers by MPs on behalf of their constituents.

ii) <u>Promoting the interests of the constituency.</u> An MP will look after the needs and problems of the constituency through speeches in parliament, committee work or personal approaches to ministers and civil servants. This sort of work might be to promote a new road, or bring new employment to the area, or to get government or European grants for the area.

The Functions of the House of Lords

<u>There were four main functions of the House of Lords prior to reform</u>

<u>and it would seem as if these four are to continue:</u>

- **Legislation**: The Lords as well as the Commons must approve all legislation but, thanks to the Parliament Acts of 1911 and 1949, the Lords do not have the power to reject legislation that has been passed by the Commons. <u>The most they can do is to delay a bill for the maximum of one year or parliamentary session</u> (2 years between 1911 and 1949). One useful legislative function of the Lords is to take some of the pressure off the House of Commons by doing the lion's share of work on non-controversial bills, private bills and delegated legislation.

- **Scrutiny**: Committees in the Lords do a lot of work in examining government policy and actions, particularly in areas where members of the Commons are not particularly interested. Most of the scrutiny of **European Union legislation** is done in the Lords.

- **Debate:** Because there is not the same pressure of business as there is in the Commons, the Lords can afford to debate important matters at leisure and in depth. The quality of debate is said to be much better in the Lords because the majority of members are older and more experienced than the average MP. And many of the peers are not professional politicians.

- **Law Court**: The House of Lords is the British equivalent of a **Supreme Court** and is the final court of appeal within the country: although it can now be out-ranked by the **European Court of Justice**. Appeals and judicial hearings in the Lords are heard by a **judicial committee** made up of between five and ten Law Lords. Evidence is taken in a small committee room but the result is announced in the House. Peers who are not law lords cannot take part.

Parliament and Legislation

Parliament is Britain's **legislature**, which means that its main job is to legislate by passing laws. A law that is passed by parliament is known as a **statute** and something that must be done by law is known as a **statutory requirement**. Laws are not just the sort of thing that are enforced by the police and the courts, they include all the rules that regulate how the country is run. Laws affect all of us in the little details of our daily life. For example, every school in the country must register all its pupils every day; that is a **statutory requirement**.

Something that it is intended should become a law is presented to parliament as **a bill**. It then goes through **the**

legislative process and, when it has been approved by both houses of parliament and signed in the name of the Queen, it becomes an **Act of Parliament** and part of **Statute Law**.

There are two kinds of bills brought before parliament, one of them divided into two sub-types:

1) Public Bills:

These are bills intended for the general good of the public as a whole. They must be presented to parliament by a member of parliament and are divided into two categories -

a) **Government Bills**: are introduced by a government minister and are the way in which a government carries out the programme for which it was elected. The bills a government intends to introduce during the course of a year are announced in the **Queen's Speech** at the **State Opening of Parliament**. After that the process of dealing with government bills is the thing which takes up most of parliament's time.

b) **Private Members' Bills (PMBs)**: are introduced by any MP (there are also **Private Peers' Bills** in the House of Lords), either **by ballot** or under the **'ten-minute rule'**. Every year, MPs who want to introduce their own bill put forward their names, and twenty of these are chosen by drawing lots. Those whose names are chosen can try to introduce their bill on the twelve Friday mornings set aside for PMBs. Alternatively, an MP who wants to introduce a bill can make a *t*en-minute speech after Question Time on Tuesday or Wednesday. Another MP can then make a ten minute speech against the bill and MPs vote to see whether the bill will be accepted. If it is the bill is discussed and dealt with on Friday mornings along with the ballot bills. So little time is set aside for PMBs that most stand no chance at all. About fifteen bills a year do become law (ten of these from the Lords) but to succeed, a PMB has to be uncontroversial and have the approval of the government.

2) Private Bills:

These are bills presented to parliament by **local authorities or private companies** to allow them to do something that is really the concern of parliament. In the past a lot of legislation was private - in the 18th and 19th centuries farmland was enclosed and the network of British canals and railways was built through a series of private bills. When the government became more involved in the way the country is run, most legislation became public rather than private and now private bills take up less than 5% of parliament's time. In recent years, however, the growing number of private ports, marinas, bridges, tram and light railway systems that are being built require private bills to set them up. There are also **hybrid bills** where the government shares a project with a private company and the bill to set up the project is a mixture of public and private. The bill to set up the Channel Tunnel is a good example of a hybrid bill.

Private bills are introduced by lawyers known as **parliamentary agents** acting for the **promoters** of the bill. The committee stage of a private bill is like a court of law with lawyers arguing the case for all sides, witnesses are called and evidence taken, with the committee of MPs acting like judge and jury.

The Consultative and Legislative Process

Consultation and Drafting

Every political party has a programme which is put forward in their election manifesto. Once a party is elected to government they have to decide when and how each part of their programme will be turned into law. Every year, well before the start of the new parliamentary session a **Cabinet committee** will decide on the legislation to be introduced in that session. The list of proposed bills will be announced in the **Queen's Speech** at the opening of the session.

The ministers and departments responsible for the various bills, together with their civil servants and advisory committees, will begin **drafting** the bill, setting out the form the proposed act will take. During the drafting process the civil servants will seek advice from lawyers, experts in that field, party policy committees etc. <u>They will also be lobbied by pressure groups and other interested parties</u>. If the group drafting the bill want to get more advice or test public opinion, they issue either a **Green Paper** or a **White Paper**:

A **Green Paper** (printed on green paper) is an outline of what is proposed, and is asking for the opinion of anyone interested in the subject. <u>It is a consultation document.</u>

A **White Paper** (on white paper) is close to what the government intends and reads like the final draft bill. It is inviting consultation but is more <u>a statement of intention</u> - rather like saying, *"Unless you can think up a very good reason, this is what we're going to do."*

In the course of consulting over proposed legislation, it may be decided that the matter is sufficiently important and controversial for the reaction of the general public to be considered. For this purpose **a public enquiry** might well be set up, with a prominent legal or political figure in the chair. The enquiry would be held in public and members of the public would be free to give their testimony to the hearing. Pressure groups and other interested parties would also give evidence and these same interested parties might choose to be legally represented during the public hearings. The findings of the enquiry would be made available to the public but would primarily be of use to those civil servants and politicians drafting the legislation.

The time taken up by consultation and drafting the bill can be as much as a year to eighteen months.

In Parliament

When the bill is drafted the minister responsible will announce the government's intention to introduce it in the Commons. This is known as **the First Reading**. It is only a formality and there is no debate. After this the bill is printed and circulated to MPs.

About two weeks later, the bill is debated by the House of Commons, the debate usually taking one day, although an important measure may take two. This is **the Second Reading**. The debate is about the principle of the bill, not the details. At the end of the debate a **division** is called (MPs vote by dividing and walking through either the **Aye lobby** or the **No lobby**). If the bill is defeated that is the end of it.

Government bills almost never fail their second reading but most private member's bills never get any further.

One of the **Commons' Standing Committees** will then consider the bill in every detail. This is **the Committee Stage**. **Amendments** can be suggested and voted on. The committee stage can take up to three months but if things are taking too long the government can propose a **guillotine**, which puts a time limit on discussions, or a **kangaroo**, which means only a selection of clauses is discussed.

What has happened in committee is passed on to the Commons at **the Report Stage**, when other last-minute amendments can be discussed. Immediately following the report stage the bill in its final form is discussed in **the Third Reading** and there is a division. But this is largely a formality and the bill is not likely to be defeated.

The bill now goes to the House of Lords and goes through all the same stages, except that the committee stage is discussed by the full house and votes take place over amendments in committee only, not over debates on the principle of the bill. If any part of the bill agreed by the Commons is rejected by the Lords, the Commons can accept the amendment or send it back for the Lords to think again. Whatever happens, the Lords cannot delay the passage of the bill for more than 12 months. Some bills start in the Lords rather than the Commons in which case all the same stages take place, but the other way around.

When a bill has passed both houses of parliament it then goes to the **Assent Office** to receive the formality of the **Royal Assent**. The Bill has become an Act. In theory, the Queen could refuse to sign an act but she is unlikely to so so because it would cause an immense constitutional crisis, with the queen accused of *"thwarting the will of the people"*. The last monarch who refused to pass an Act was Queen Anne who refused the Militia Bill in 1707.

Financial Legislation

Not all legislation is about passing laws. Some of the most important debates in the House of Commons are about how much money the government spends and how it raises that money. Years ago it was parliament's control over what is known as **the money supply** that helped parliament to keep a check on the king - *"Unless you do what we say"*, they would tell him, *"we shall not allow you to raise any taxes."* For hundreds of years, by law since 1911, the House of Commons has been the only body allowed to deal with the money supply, the Lords cannot hold up financial legislation for more than one month.

The first thing the government has to do is to decide how much money it needs. In 'the spending round', all the spending departments of government submit **estimates** to the **Treasury** of how much money they think they will need in the coming year. The **Chief Secretary to the Treasury** is the cabinet minister in charge of the estimates. He considers

- the total amount of money asked for in the estimates

- decides how much the government can afford

- and then shares out the money between the different departments.

- He might well ask some departments to make cuts in their estimates. If there is an argument between the Chief Secretary and a department over the size of an estimate the final say is in the hands of a cabinet committee with the nickname of **the Star Chamber**.

There are two parts to the **Finance Bill**. First there is legislation to approve all spending according to the estimates. Once there was a time when each department's estimates were debated separately. But nowadays all the estimates are voted on together, except when spending is passed to other bodies like local government. Secondly there is **the Budget**, in which the Chancellor of the Exchequer says how he is going to raise the money in taxes. Until 1993, and again since 1997, the two parts of the Finance Bill have been dealt with separately:

1) the estimates are discussed in the November **Autumn Statement**

2) the **Budget** is in the following March or April.

It was Norman Lamont, when he was Chancellor, who decided that both statements should be made at the same time, in the autumn. Bringing the two statements together would make it clear to government ministers that they cannot have low taxation and high public spending at the same time. For a time after 1993 the Budget was in November, with the Finance Bill following in January but the two parts separated again under Gordon Brown as Chancellor.

The Finance Bill is debated at length, the committee stage for taxation measures taking place on the floor of the House of Commons, in what is known as a **Committee of the Whole House**; more routine matters are discussed by a normal standing committee.

The Finance Bill takes longer than any other parliamentary process, requiring anything up to four months to pass through parliament, even though the House of Lords has <u>no power to amend or delay a Money Bill for more than a month</u>. During that time there are plenty of opportunities for the issues to be debated at length by the House of Commons.

It is very rare for major amendments to be made to a Finance Bill: the defeat of the government over VAT on fuel in December 1995 was the first defeat on a major budget measure for eighteen years. Such a defeat can only happen when the government's majority is seriously reduced.

Secondary Legislation

By secondary legislation we mean legislation that parliament knows about and approves but which is not passed by parliament itself.

Legislative Devolution:

This is a new factor since the introduction of the devolved parliament in Scotland and the devolved assembly in Wales. The advent of the devolved bodies means that there are assemblies other than the Westminster parliament capable of passing legislation. Mostly the laws passed in Edinburgh or Cardiff are secondary legislation, having all the characteristics of <u>delegated legislation</u>. However, the second referendum on Scottish devolution, which granted the Scottish Parliament the right to raise taxation independent of Westminster, means that Edinburgh has gained the right to pass its own **primary legislation** in the form of financial legislation.

Delegated Legislation:

There are some laws which must be passed but which are not dealt with by parliament for one reason or another. In these cases the government delegates the right to make laws to other bodies or people:

1) There are local matters that are <u>too trivial</u> or which require <u>too much local knowledge</u> for parliament to deal with them. Westminster cannot be bothered about rules against walking on the grass or dropping litter in the park. Nor do they know which stretches of road should have a 40 mph speed limit, or where there should be a pelican crossing.

2) There are certain nationalised, or privatised, public services which need to make laws for the people who use those services. But <u>they are **operational rules** concerning things about which civil servants and politicians know nothing</u>. Government ministers and senior civil servants cannot be bothered about the age at which children pay half fare on the bus; or what the penalty should be for tampering with a gas meter.

3) There are laws that are general but the **detailed application** of those laws may need to change for one reason or another. For example, there is a general law that chemists should charge for prescriptions but the amount that is charged changes over time. It would obviously be wasteful to go through the entire legislative process in order to increase the price of prescriptions by 25p. <u>There has to be a way to change the **technical details** of a law without referring the matter back to parliament.</u>

For all these examples parliament grants ministers, civil servants, local authorities, industry regulators etc. the power to make **by-laws**, rules and regulations. The parliamentary authority to make these laws is known as **a statutory instrument**. About 2000 statutory instruments are issued every year; the more important of them, especially those known as **orders in council**, needing later approval by parliament.

European Legislation:

The laws of the European Community are made by the **Council of Ministers**, with the help of the **Commission** and with some scrutiny by the **European Parliament**. The British parliament has no say except through ministers, but draft legislation can be discussed by special committees of either the Lords or the Commons, and they can recommend what they think the minister should do. According to the treaty that Britain signed when joining the EC in 1972, <u>European laws are accepted automatically as if they had been passed by the British parliament.</u>

Laws agreed by the **Council of Ministers** are put into proper form by the **Commission** and then released to member countries as **legal instruments**. About 12,000 **legal instruments** are issued every year, although most are about very unimportant details. There are five types of legal instruments but only two are really important:

- **Regulations** - which become law as soon as they are issued, and in the form in which they are worded.

- **Directives** - are laws that are less detailed than regulations. Member governments are told what EC policy is but <u>each government chooses their own way of meeting that policy.</u>

During the year the Council of Ministers will issue about 400 important regulations and about 80 directives.

Revision exercise 6:

If you were an interest or pressure group wishing to influence government legislation,

where, when and how would you set about trying to exert your influence?

CHAPTER SIX

Government and the civil service

At the heart and centre of government is **the executive**. This is the part of the political structure which <u>decides policy, makes decisions, draws up proposed laws, directs the economy and sees that all aspects of the country are run smoothly</u>. And at the heart of the executive is the body of leading politicians and ministers which, for the sake of convenience, we call '<u>the government</u>'.

. In countries such as the United States, they have what is called the **Separation of Powers**, which means that the executive is separate from the legislature, and the judiciary is separate from both. In the United States, the <u>President and his government</u> are very often from a different party than the one which controls <u>Congress</u>. This, it is believed, strengthens democracy because it prevents the concentration of power in the hands of one person or just a few people.

In Britain we have no real separation of powers since, in **parliamentary government**, although it is not legally required, members of the government are drawn from Parliament, largely because ministers are supposed to be answerable to Parliament for their actions and Parliament wants them to be there to explain themselves. If the prime minister wants to appoint someone to government who is not an MP they are either found a safe constituency or they are given a peerage to bring them into the House of Lords. Members of the government can be chosen from either the Commons or the Lords but the most important ministers are members of the House of Commons.

The government is made up of:

1. **The Prime Minister**

2. A **Cabinet** of Senior Ministers, usually **Secretaries of State**.

3. Junior Ministers, **Under-Secretaries of State,** or **Ministers of State**.

4. Holders of junior office, such as **Parliamentary Private Secretaries**, who are often unpaid for their extra duties and who act as general dogsbodies and bag-carriers for their ministers.

When **government whips** and **law officers** are taken into account, governments are quite large, usually containing over one hundred members. It is useful to the prime minister to have as large a government as possible because it keeps possible rebels quiet. Members of a government are bound by **collective responsibility**, meaning that no member of a government should criticise the policies of that government, once policies have been agreed. Government membership silences critics who might cause trouble if they were left on the back benches.

There was a time when government ministers were chosen by the monarch, but that changed with the growth in democracy. All laws are passed by the House of Commons and it is important to the government that it should be able to get all its proposed laws passed. <u>The government is therefore formed by anyone who is certain to command majority support in the House of Commons.</u> This means that <u>the leader of the largest party in the Commons after a general election almost automatically becomes the prime minister</u>, and the ministers making up the government are chosen from that largest party.

If no one party wins the election, or if a party loses its majority during the course of a parliament, then arrangements must be made with other parties to ensure that the government continues to keep the support of the Commons, if there is not to be another general election. Sometimes that could mean choosing government ministers from more than one party and forming what is called a **coalition government**. Coalitions can also be formed in times of national emergency, as at the time of the two World Wars.

The second largest party in the Commons after an election becomes the official **Opposition** - a sort of alternative government or 'government in waiting'. The leader of that party becomes the **Leader of the Opposition** (a paid position) and forms a **Shadow Government** with party spokespersons mirroring (or 'shadowing') all government ministers.

Membership of the government changes throughout its life, with those who have done well being promoted and those who have done badly being demoted, in periodic **re-shuffles** of the government team made by the prime minister. The government itself lasts for the life of a parliament. But a government might have to resign and call an election before its five years are up, if it is defeated in the Commons on a **motion of confidence**.

The Prime Minister

The **Prime Minister** is **head of government**, as against the Queen who is **head of state**. The office of prime minister was largely created by accident, simply because the first Hanoverian kings (George I and George II) were German and did not speak enough English to chair meetings of ministers. Robert Walpole, who was **First Lord of the Treasury** (a post still officially held by the prime minister), was chosen to chair cabinet meetings on behalf of the king. At first the prime minister was not thought of as being more important than any other minister: he was said to be *primus inter pares* (first among equals). But since then, and particularly in this century, the prime minister has become very important indeed - head of government, leader of the governing party and representing the party and government in the eyes of the country.

In theory, the monarch can choose anyone at all to become prime minister but in fact there is a convention (a way things have always been done) which says that the choice will automatically fall on the leader of the party which has won the general election. The prime minister is therefore chosen by the party first and the country second. In recent years there have been those who have said that general elections in Britain were getting like presidential elections in America, because a general election is seen to be more about choosing the next prime minister than about choosing 659 members of parliament.

In the nineteenth century, prime ministers were often chosen from the House of Lords, but the last peer to serve as prime minister was Lord Salisbury (1895-1902). Today, it is unthinkable that the prime minister should not be a member of the Commons. When a peer (Lord Home) was chosen as leader of the Conservative Party in 1963 he had to give up his peerage and fight an election, as Sir Alec Douglas-Home, before he became prime minister.

The prime minister's duties and powers are largely based on the royal prerogative and are really those duties and powers formerly held by the monarch but now exercised by the government in the name of the monarch.

The Prime Minister (PM):

- Appoints all members of the government, decides on the relative importance of those ministers and can later dismiss, promote or demote the ministers he or she has appointed.

- In making these appointments, the PM also decides the structure of government by deciding on the number and responsibilities of the various government departments. As well as choosing government ministers the PM has a large say in the appointment of people to the most important positions in national life, such as senior civil servants, as well as nominating people for the creation of peers and the award of honours.

- Directs and organises the government through leading and co-ordinating policy and strategy; chairing the Cabinet and cabinet committees.

- The PM also has a direct influence on economic, foreign and defence policy in association with the relevant secretaries of state and is personally responsible for the agencies of national security.

- As **head of the Civil Service** the PM makes the final decisions on appointments, organisation and practice.

- Represents the government in parliament, particularly in answering questions at **Prime Minister's Question Time** (answering about 1000 questions each session). The PM controls the House of Commons as leader of the majority party; makes statements to the House and may intervene in important debates.

- The PM also has the sole right to decide when Parliament should be dissolved and an election called.

- The PM is the national leader, representing the country internationally in receiving visiting statesmen, leading official visits abroad, signing treaties and representing the United Kingdom on bodies such as the European Council. The PM is constantly appearing in the press and on tv and radio to present the views of party, government or country.

- In the last resort the PM can declare war, as Mrs Thatcher did over the Falklands, John Major did in the Gulf War with Iraq and Tony Blair did in the Kosovo dispute.

The Cabinet

Despite the importance of the prime minister, government in the UK is not by a single person but through **collective government** in the form of an executive committee known as the **Cabinet**. The cabinet lies at the heart of the government and is responsible for:

- the <u>formation of a common government policy</u>

- <u>co-ordinating the work of government departments</u>

- <u>approving decisions made by individual cabinet ministers</u>; e.g. the cabinet always discusses and approves the Budget before the Chancellor makes his speech.

The cabinet meets at least once a week - usually on Thursday mornings for about three hours. Meetings are chaired by the prime minister who has also set the **agenda** for what is to be discussed. There is no vote at the end of the discussion, <u>the prime minister will sum up the majority opinion of the meeting</u>. A member of the cabinet may say what they like about government policy during a cabinet meeting but once it has been approved as government policy all cabinet members must support that policy, whether they agree with it or not. If they disagree with government policy they must either keep quiet or resign: this is the doctrine of **collective responsibility**. Because the cabinet should always appear united, what happens in cabinet meetings is secret and the **minutes** of the meeting and other cabinet papers <u>are kept secret for thirty years</u> before being released to the public.

The minutes of cabinet meetings are kept by the **Cabinet Secretary,** the most senior civil servant and effective head of the civil service. He is assisted by the **Cabinet Office**, or **Secretariat**, consisting of about 35 senior civil servants who are seconded from other government departments.

<u>The Cabinet Office:</u>

1. <u>prepares agendas and discussion papers</u>

2. takes minutes

3. circulates documents

4. plans business and implements decisions for the meetings not only of the cabinet but for the very many cabinet committees.

Meetings of the full cabinet are too large to make effective decisions themselves and in any case there is far too much business to be dealt with in any detail during a three-hour meeting. The full cabinet normally just agrees with decisions that have already been made by one of the many much smaller **Cabinet Committees**. There are about thirty **standing cabinet committees** dealing with different policy areas, each with memberships of between six and sixteen ministers. As well as these, there are over a hundred *ad hoc* cabinet committees set up to deal with specific issues. The most important cabinet committees are chaired by the prime minister, the others by senior cabinet ministers such as the Deputy Prime Minister or Chancellor of the Exchequer.

The full cabinet usually consists of about 22 members apart from the prime minister and there are 22 salaries of cabinet rank for the prime minister to distribute. At intervals there will be a move to reduce the size of the cabinet but it soon climbs back up again to settle around 23. The actual membership can alter depending on the wishes of the prime minister, but always included are:

Principal Officers of State - Chancellor of the Exchequer, Foreign Secretary, Home Secretary.

Treasury Ministers - the prime minister (as First Lord of the Treasury) and the Chancellor, of course, together with the Chief Secretary to the Treasury.

Secretaries of State from the spending departments - Agriculture, Defence, Education & Employment, Environment, Health, National Heritage, Social Security, Trade & Industry, Transport.

Law Officers - Lord Chancellor, Attorney-General, Solicitor-General.

National Secretaries of State - Scottish Secretary, Welsh Secretary, Northern Ireland Secretary.

Non-departmental ministers - Lord President of Council, Chancellor of the Duchy of Lancaster, Lord Privy Seal, Paymaster-General, Minister without portfolio, Chief Whip.

Ministers and Departments

The government is divided up into units known as **departments, offices** or **ministries**. They vary in size from the small (Welsh Office, with 2,400 staff) to the very large (Defence, with 140,000 staff). Each of these has:

1. **Secretary of State** as its political head to decide on policy, who will in turn be supported by:

2. one or more **Ministers of State**

3. and one or more **Under-Secretaries of State**.

Most of the staff within departments are <u>permanent civil</u> <u>servants who administer the work of the departments and</u> <u>carry out the wishes of the politicians</u>.

There are three major offices of state

The holders of these offices are regarded as the three most senior members of the government after the prime minister. They are:

The Foreign and Commonwealth Office - dealing with foreign relations policy, diplomatic relations with foreign and Commonwealth governments, participation in the United Nations and NATO and liaison with the European Union. At the head is the **Foreign Secretary** assisted by four Ministers of State with special responsibilities, such as <u>Overseas</u> <u>Development</u> or <u>Europe</u>.

The Home Office - is responsible for law and order with overall responsibility for justice, the police, the penal system, immigration and public safety. The **Home Secretary** is also <u>directly in charge of the Metropolitan Police</u>. Again, there are several Home Office Ministers below the Home Secretary, each responsible for one particular section, such as <u>Prisons</u> or <u>Immigration</u>.

The Treasury - raises and allocates the money spent by government, liaises with the City and Bank of England and <u>decides on economic and financial policies for the country</u>. The Treasury is possibly the most influential government department because it finds the money that is spent by the other departments. There are three senior Treasury Ministers who are always cabinet ministers:

- the prime minister as **First Lord of the Treasury**

- the **Chancellor of the Exchequer** who is the secretary of state at the Treasury and in overall charge

- the **Chief Secretary to the Treasury** who deals with departmental estimates and allocating money to the departments.

- Below these three there is an **Economics Secretary**, a **Financial Secretary** and two Ministers of State.

There are at least ten **"spending ministries"**

so-called because they spend rather than raise money and are always in dispute with the Treasury over the amount of money they need.

It was in the 1960s that the government attempted to reduce the number of ministries by grouping several together into large departments, bringing a number of Ministers of State together under one Secretary of State. But the number, size and responsibilities of departments have changed ever since, according to the thinking of the prime minister of the day as to the structure of government:

- Departments and Ministries can be abolished, merged or transferred to make new, larger departments. e.g. In 1995 'training' was moved from the **Department of Trade and Industry**, the **Department of Employment** was abolished and these responsibilities joined with 'education' to make a **Department for Education and Employment.**

- Departments can be divided to make two or more new departments. e.g. In 1989, the **Department of Health and Social Security,** formed in 1968 when the fashion was for large departments, was divided into two to form the **Department of Health** and the **Department of Social Security**.

Law Officers

- The **Lord Chancellor's Department** (**Lord Chancellor**): is responsible for the administration of the Law - lawyers, the legal system and the courts.

- **Law Officers' Department** (**Attorney-General** and **Solicitor-General**): is responsible for enforcing the criminal law, as well as providing legal advice to the government and acting as barrister or solicitor in court cases brought by the government.

- **Lord Advocate's Department** (**Lord Advocate** and **Solicitor-General for Scotland**): has the same functions as the Law Officers' Department but under Scottish law.

Ministers without departmental responsibilities

There are a number of ministerial positions which have historic importance but which no longer have any specific duties:

- **President of the Council** - formerly had duties connected with the Privy Council but is now usually the title given to the Leader of the House of Commons.

104

Sometimes known as the Lord President of Council, the 'Lord' is dropped if the holder is a woman, as was the case in the Blair government.

- **Lord Privy Seal** - originally the keeper of the Seal which was used to seal important state papers and part of the <u>Privy Council Office</u>, but now with no real duties except to act as Leader of the House of Lords.

- **Chancellor of the Duchy of Lancaster** - there are still some duties concerned with administering the Duchy's business but they are very few and the real importance of the position is now to act as the minister in charge of the Office of Public Service and Science in the Cabinet Office, responsible for consumer policy, the Citizen's Charter and 'open government'.

- **Paymaster-General** - responsible, in theory, for paying out all money granted by Parliament but in fact the position is really as a figurehead for the P-G's Office since there are no administrative duties. The post is used to give added weight and numbers to the Treasury team in negotiations with spending ministers.

- **Minister without Portfolio** - the name given to anyone the prime minister wants to have in government without their having to look after a department.

These positions are used by the prime minister for a variety of purposes:

i) <u>To give a place in government to someone important in the governing party.</u> For example, in the Thatcher and Major governments, the **Chairman of the Conservative Party**, was regularly included in the cabinet as <u>a minister without portfolio.</u>

ii) <u>To handle a special responsibility below departmental level,</u> as was the case in 1995 when the **Chancellor of the Duchy of Lancaster** first assumed responsibilities for <u>Public Affairs and Science.</u>

iii) <u>To act as spokesman in the Commons when the Secretary of State is in the Lords.</u> For example, when Lord Carrington was Foreign Secretary (1979-82), questions about foreign affairs were answered in the Commons by Sir Ian Gilmour as **Lord Privy Seal**.

iv) <u>To act as Leader of the House.</u> This is applicable to both the Commons and Lords. As has been said, the **President of the Council**, is usually **Leader of the House of Commons** and the **Lord Privy Seal**, is **Leader of the House of Lords**. <u>The Leader of the House arranges the smooth operation of parliament, through agreeing a week's timetable in advance, deciding on subjects for debate, printing order papers etc.</u>

The Whips:

The Chief Government Whip is a member of the cabinet and is an important member of the government, having an official house in Downing Street (no. 12), like the Prime Minister and Chancellor. Together with the other members of the Whips' Office, the Chief Whip is responsible for <u>discipline in the party - encouraging MPs to vote on important issues; punishing those who do not vote or vote against their party; listening to what the MPs in the party are saying and keeping</u>

the government informed as to party morale and the chance of party rebellions. If the life of the government depends on a majority in the Commons then the Chief Whip's job is to keep the government alive.

The Civil Service

The Civil Service is the government's **bureaucracy**. Government departments are run by ministers who are elected politicians, but they are administered by professional and permanent paid officials who are the civil service. Civil servants can be divided into:

- industrial civil servants - people who work in government workshops or factories, or who work as drivers, messengers etc.

- scientific and technical staff - staff in government research laboratories or providers of specialised services, like architects.

- general civil servants - who provide the general bureaucratic and administrative services. Most are clerical or managerial staff, distributed in government offices throughout the country.

The civil servants who most concern the student of politics are the **administrative grade civil servants** who are based in the large government departments in **Whitehall**. They are very few in number (less than 1% of non-industrial civil servants) but very important and influential.

These senior civil servants:

- advise ministers on policy

- prepare and draft discussion documents and legislation

- act as a secretariat for ministerial meetings

- prepare ministerial answers to questions from parliament or the public

- implement government decisions.

The civil service head of each government department is the **Permanent Secretary**, beneath whom in descending order there are:

1 **Deputy Secretaries**

2 **Under Secretaries**

3 **Assistant Secretaries**

4 **Senior Principals**

5 and **Principals**.

The effective head of the civil service is **the Cabinet Secretary**, who is the equivalent of the prime minister's permanent secretary.

Traditionally, the Civil Service in Britain was known for being three things. It was:

- **Permanent** - Unlike ministers, civil servants do not change at election time. A permanent civil service leads to experienced civil servants and continuity between governments.

108

- **Neutral** - Civil servants do not allow their political opinions to influence what they do and they carry out the government's policies whatever the party and whether they agree with it or not. Civil servants cannot stand for election, nor take an open part in party political activity.

- **Anonymous** - Since no one is supposed to know who civil servants are, or what advice they give, civil servants can give clear impartial advice without fear of that the public might say.

Civil servants have become less neutral and anonymous in recent years, but that is a separate issue.

The Changing Civil Service

Since 1990, much of the administration of government has been handed over from government departments to **agencies** set up under the '**Next Steps**' programme. By the time the end of the Next Steps programme was announced in 1997 a total of 138 agencies had been set up, with another 50 planned. 76% of all civil servants (more than 380,000) are employed by these **agencies** that are headed by appointed chief executives rather than in traditional **government departments** headed by elected government ministers. It is expected that the number of civil servants employed within the agency structure by the year 2000 will be over 450,000, more than 80% of the whole Civil Service.

All government departments are affected in this way, some more so than others. Social Security, for example, has the **Benefits Agency** and the **Child Support Agency** carrying out specialised functions for the department. Like the

Treasury, Agriculture and Environment, <u>Social Security has six agencies under its wing</u>. The Defence Ministry has no fewer than <u>21 agencies</u>, ranging from the <u>Defence Procurement Agency</u> which buys weapons for the forces, to the <u>Meteorological Office</u> which produces weather forecasts.

<u>There are areas of concern over the existence of these agencies.</u>

- **Expense. Chief executives of the agencies** are paid much more than senior civil servants. For example, <u>the chief executive of the Prison Service was paid a salary of £133,280, while someone on a similar civil service grade had a salary of £73,000.</u>

- **Accountability.** The agencies and their <u>chief executives are not accountable to parliament or the electorate</u>, as government ministers and their departments used to be. When the <u>Child Support Agency</u> proved to be so ineffective that it had virtually collapsed, questions in the House of Commons produced a reply from the minister that "*it has nothing to do with me*". Much the same answer was given over mistakes made by the Prison Service. In three days there was <u>a suicide in one prison, a riot in another and three dangerous criminals escaped from a third.</u> When Michael Howard, as Home Secretary, was asked why it was that the head of the Prison Service agency had been asked to resign but the Home Secretary was going to carry on as if nothing had happened, Howard said that <u>the executive of an agency is responsible for operational decisions while a minister is only responsible for policy.</u> Members of the public could once challenge a government minister over the actions of his or her department through their MP. This

110

is no longer the case because <u>there is no one in parliament accountable for the actions of these agencies.</u>

Quangos and other unelected bodies

The agencies are only one example of the way that elected bodies which were accountable to the public are being replaced by **quangos** and <u>other bodies that are appointed rather than elected</u> and therefore do not have to answer to anyone. When Mrs Thatcher came to power in 1979 she promised to end the quangos set up by the Labour government in the 1970s. In fact, instead of ending the quangos, she multiplied their number:

i) by abolishing whole sections of local government and setting up unelected bodies to run services previously provided by local councils, like bus services and emptying the bins

ii) by encouraging schools to <u>opt out of local authority control</u> to become **grant maintained**, and <u>National Health Service hospitals</u> to become **Trusts**.

Most quangos meet in secret and only a third need to have their accounts audited. Also, the appointment of executives to quangos becomes a form of political patronage for whichever political party is in power and able to make appointments.

111

Revision exercise 7:

Be very clear as to the difference between government departments, quangos and government agencies. For each of them ask the questions:-

Who works there and who is in charge of policy and administrative decisions?

Who is responsible if anything goes wrong?

To whom or to what are the workers accountable?

CHAPTER SEVEN

Government Processes

Policy making

The way in which governments and political parties decide on their policies is very complicated. There are two kinds of policy which concern us:

1) **General policy** - these are the policies based on a party's **ideology** (what a party believes) and which affect their overall view of society and how that society should be run.

   In this way <u>the Conservatives would claim to be in favour of private enterprise, competition, low taxes, law and order etc.</u>

   And <u>the Labour Party would claim to be in favour of full employment, caring for the less well off, treating people on an equal basis and so on.</u>

   These policies will be laid out in the party's **election manifesto** but they are well known and do not change much over the years.

2) **Issue-related policies** - these are the policies that are produced in answer to the various issues which concern the electorate. For example, <u>if the public is worried about</u>

education, the parties evolve policies to deal with education. These specific policies are what elections are fought over and these are the policies that will be followed by an elected government in deciding on legislation.

There are many factors influencing the formation of policy:

Public opinion - Politicians get to know what the people think through various channels:

- When an issue is taken up by the **media**, especially the tabloid newspapers. This not only lets the politicians know that the public is concerned but regular mentions in the press increase the strength of public opinion.

- Increased support for, and activity by, the relevant **pressure groups**.

- **Letters to MPs** and government ministers, and sometimes a **"lobby"** of parliament, when large numbers of people turn up at the Houses of Parliament and demand to see their MPs. Also, sometimes, **petitions**.

- **How people vote** in elections. The environment turned into an important issue when the Green Party increased its share of the vote in the 1989 European elections.

Insider Pressure Groups - Powerful and influential groups like the CBI, the trade unions or important industries like building or transport, will be able to talk to ministers and civil servants, helping to put across their own policy views.

Party opinion - Members of the party outside parliament are always passing information back to the centre, telling the leadership what **grassroot opinion** says ought to be done.

Parties also have groups who meet to discuss party policy, with the hope of influencing the leadership. The Conservatives have groups like the <u>Bow Group</u>, or the <u>One Nation Group.</u> Labour has the <u>Fabian Society</u>, or the <u>Tribune Group</u>.

Think Tanks - Groups or committees of university people and other academics, who develop policy ideas, often from a particular point of view. The so-called "Middle Way" or "Third Way" which typified the thinking of the Blair government in 1997 was developed by the independent think-tank <u>Demos</u>.

Public Enquiries and Royal Commissions - These are long investigations, often run by lawyers, which look into issues the public is worried about, and make recommendations that can become policy. <u>Recent important commissions have looked at things like local government and criminal justice.</u>

Civil Servants - The job of civil servants is to take the various policy ideas that are around and turn turn them into <u>policy statements</u> that suit the politicians but are also capable of being put into practice. There is a **policy unit** in the **Prime Minister's Office**. <u>The civil service help to prevent extreme policies by reminding politicians of what it is practical to do.</u>

Forming a Government

Immediately after a general election, as soon as the result is known, <u>the leader of the party with most seats in the House of Commons</u> will be sent for by the Queen and asked <u>to become prime minister and to form a government</u>. Forming that government will be the PM's first job and it will take a long time. The most important posts, the **Foreign Secretary**,

Chancellor of the Exchequer, the **Home Secretary** and the other members of the **Cabinet** will be chosen very quickly but the **junior ministers and parliamentary private secretaries** will only be appointed over a period of many days, because the government will finally have over a hundred members.

The prime minister has a free choice in selecting a government and, in an ideal world, the PM would choose friends, close colleagues, MPs who think the same way and people with lots of experience. But there are a number of factors that limit the amount of choice a prime minister has:

- There are a number of government posts that have to be filled by certain kinds of people - the Lord Chancellor, Attorney-General and other law officers have to be lawyers; the Leader of the House of Lords has to be a peer; and the Secretaries of State for Scotland and Wales should preferably be MPs for Scottish or Welsh constituencies.

- The ministers should have some experience, either as a junior minister (or as **shadow ministers** if they have been in opposition).

- The prime minister should be looking out for future senior ministers by promoting talented newcomers into junior positions.

- The different factions in the party - **left** and **right, wets** and **dries, Euro-sceptics** and **Euro-enthusiasts** - should all be represented in the government so as not to split the party.

- Some party members will need a reward for the work they have done for the party and for the prime minister - maybe they supported the PM in the leadership campaign, or they have worked very hard for the party during the election.

- Possible troublemakers in the party should be brought into government because they will not be able to cause trouble if they are bound by **collective responsibility**.

All these things are true of a prime minister's first government but, of course, the PM will change that government over time to keep it from getting stale. These **reshuffles** take place at least once a year, while if a minister should be removed through death, dismissal or resignation, the PM will not just replace the minister who has gone but will take the opportunity to move quite a few ministers around. There are a number of reasons for these changes:

- The prime minister can promote a successful junior minister to a senior post, or a new, young MP who has impressed colleagues (especially the Whips) can be tried out in a junior position to test their potential.

- Ministers who are inefficient, incompetent or who have made too many mistakes can be removed or demoted.

- After a couple of years, when the prime minister is feeling secure, those MPs who were given places in the government to keep them quiet, or for the sake of party unity, can be got rid of and replaced by the sort of people that the PM finds more sympathetic.

All these things are also true of the **Shadow Cabinet** and shadow ministers chosen by the **Leader of the Opposition** and the leaders of other opposition parties. But the Labour Party, when in opposition, <u>has its Shadow Cabinet elected by the Party Conference</u>, although the party leader decides which posts they will fill and the leader can appoint shadow ministers who were not elected by the party.

~~Rear~~ ~~Po~~ sition

The House of Commons is divided into two. On one side is the largest party, forming the government, while on the other side are **all the other parties**, <u>forming the opposition</u>. The largest of the opposition parties becomes **the official Opposition** and has a leader, **the Leader of the Opposition**, who is officially recognised and paid a salary by parliament to lead opposition to the government.

<u>The official Opposition hope to be the government after the next election</u> so they form a **shadow government**, with the Leader of the Opposition being a sort of <u>shadow prime minister</u> and with <u>shadow spokespersons covering all the main ministerial positions</u>, so that we have a shadow chancellor, a shadow home secretary, a shadow education secretary and so on. All the minor parties on the opposition benches will have shadow spokespersons but, with these parties having so few members of parliament, one MP has to shadow several ministers at once. In most parties the spokespersons are appointed by the party leader but <u>in the Labour Party members of the Shadow Cabinet are elected by party members at the annual Conference</u> although the party leader actually appoints them to their positions and the leader is allowed to make some personal appointments from MPs who were not elected by **Conference**.

Parliament had a saying, 'The duty of the Opposition is to oppose, anything and everything.' The situation where two parties are always arguing against each other is known as **confrontational politics** and it is encouraged by the way that the House of Commons is arranged, with the two sides facing one another from opposite benches. It is noticeable that in the Scottish Parliament and Welsh Assembly, where there is no obvious opposition party because of proportional representation, the seating is much more open and non-confrontational.

Within a confrontational system there are a variety of ways in which the opposition can oppose the government:

• By challenging legislation, through speaking in debates and voting on the second and third reading of bills.

• By asking questions, at Question Time in the chamber, or through written questions to ministers, or through membership of a **select committee**.

• Opposition members can use delaying tactics, such as calling for frequent votes on trivial issues, or by keeping on talking until the time given over to that measure has run out.

• **Opposition Days:** on twenty days each year the opposition parties can choose what the House of Commons will discuss. On 17 days the choice is that of the second largest party (Conservative in the 1997 parliament) while the other three days are given over to the third largest party (usually Liberal Democrats).

• **Confidence motions:** the opposition parties can call **a Vote of No Confidence** which, if the government lose it, requires their resignation. This obviously has no point if the government has a large majority, but if the majority is small they could well lose. The Labour government under James Callaghan, who did not have a majority, lost a vote of no confidence in March 1979, causing the general election that was won by Mrs Thatcher.

- Public and press relations: the opposition parties will do all they can to oppose the government in the eyes of the general public - through the media, public meetings, press conferences, publicity etc.

Despite the role of the opposition parties and the atmosphere of confrontation, most of the business in parliament is carried on by agreement. There are regular meetings between the whips of the various parties and research has shown that only about 20% of all bills are actually opposed at the second reading. The real danger to governments is often not the opposition but disagreements within their own party, such as the disagreements over Europe within the Conservative Party.

Ministerial Responsibility

Government ministers are supposed:

- To make policy in their departments

- To manage the working of their departments

- To introduce and guide through parliament legislation made by their departments.

- To represent their departments' interests in Cabinet and in relations with the media, pressure groups and other outside bodies.

Ministers are supposed to answer for what they do. This is **ministerial responsibility** and means that ministers are accountable for their actions to -

- The Prime Minister and fellow-ministers in the government

- Their party, in and outside parliament

- The people, through parliament.

Ministers are accountable through:

- **Informal contacts and letters** from MPs, pressure groups, lobbyists and other interested parties.

- **The media**. The minister is always in the public eye and will appear in the press and on radio and television.

- **Parliamentary questions**, there are something like 15,000 questions, both written and spoken, put to ministers by MPs every month.

- **Debates in Parliament**, in which ministers must propose and defend any bills put forward by their departments.

- **Standing Committees**, in which bills supported by ministers are discussed and altered, sentence by sentence.

- **Select Committees**, which examine the work of government departments and can order a minister to appear before them to explain his/her actions.

- **The Ombudsman**, or <u>Parliamentary Commissioner for Administration</u>, to whom the public can complain about administrative faults by government departments or agencies.

Since 1980, government departments have given up many of their responsibilities. For example, <u>schools have opted-out of government control to become grant-maintained</u>; and <u>the NHS has turned to self-governing hospitals and budget-holding doctors</u>. Changes like these mean that ministers at the departments of Education and Health have very little left to say about the day-to-day running of the education and health services. Many public services have been privatised and are in the hands of private firms, while the "**Next Steps**" programme has <u>replaced the work done by Civil Service departments with lots of semi-independent agencies</u>. In 1997 it was said that well over a third of the money spent by government was spent by agencies and quangos over which ministers have very little direct financial control.

With the power to run things taken away from them, ministers do no more than make policy, leaving the operation of services to the agencies, this casts doubt on the idea of <u>ministerial responsibility</u>. In the past, civil servants were anonymous, and <u>a minister was personally accountable for the work of his/her department and the civil servants in it</u>. If anything went wrong or a serious mistake was made, <u>the minister was expected to resign,</u> even if the mistake was made by one of his/her officials, without his/her approval. Today, with named agencies in charge of operational matters, ministers are far more likely to blame other people rather than accept the blame themselves. Vernon Bogdanor, Reader in Politics at Oxford University, has said that ministerial responsibility has been turned right round, "<u>Instead of the minister taking the blame for the misjudgment of his or her officials, his or her officials must now take the blame for the misjudgments of their minister.</u>"

The Ombudsman

The word 'ombudsman' is Swedish and means '*a grievance man*'. In Sweden and Denmark the ombudsman began as a someone to whom individuals could take their complaints about bureaucratic mistakes or the errors of government. These complaints the ombudsman would then investigate; seeking to put things right if the administration was found to be at fault.

In 1967, the post of **Parliamentary Commissioner for Administration (PCA)** was created; the PCA, or ombudsman, being assisted by a staff of between sixty and ninety civil servants and supervised by a nine-member select committee. The ombudsman himself (there have not as yet been any women appointed to the position) is appointed by the prime minister with the advice of the Lord Chancellor and, since 1977, in consultation with the PCA Committee.

The idea of someone being responsible for complaints against maladministration was later extended beyond central government and ombudsmen were appointed to deal with Northern Ireland (1969), the National Health Service (1973), Local Government in England and Wales (1974) and Local

Government in Scotland (1976). These later appointments have wider powers than the PCA but they are all seen as servants of parliament rather than servants of the public. There is no ombudsman to investigate complaints against the police, nor the armed services.

Members of the public are not allowed to approach the PCA directly themselves but must go through their constituency MP. This is not true for the ombudsmen for either National Health or Local Government, who can be approached directly. The ombudsman receives around 1000 complaints each year.

i) The ombudsman must not replace a law court or tribunal.

ii) No investigation of the police or armed services is allowed.

iii) Only 14% of quangos can be investigated by the ombudsman.

Revision exercise 8:

There is no mechanism by which the ombudsman can ensure that any of his recommendations are carried out and government departments are free to ignore the ombudsman's decisions. In what ways do you think that the position of Ombudsman can be strengthened and improved?

CHAPTER EIGHT

Local Government

The Structure of Local Government

Local government began in the last century as a series of **municipal boards** set up at local level in the new big cities of the industrial revolution to deal with things like street lighting, the poor law, sanitation, water supply and so on. In **1888** the **Local Government Act** brought all these boards together, along with some newer institutions like the school boards, to create a system of councils for the whole country.

Local government exists to supply services to the public, in order that:

- The people know that the services they need are controlled by locally elected councillors, to whom they can easily take their problems, rather than controlled from a distant parliament in London.

- Councillors, who are local people themselves, will know how to provide the types of services that are best suited to that area.

The list of services provided by local councils is very long but it includes:

- **fire, police, education, housing, roads, planning, refuse collection and disposal**, social services, parks, sports centres, museums, libraries, recreational services, transport.

Many of these services, like education and housing, <u>are national services whose provision is required by central government</u> but which, for historic reasons and ease of management, have been provided by local government.

After 1888 local government was largely provided by **two tiers** of councils. The first tier was formed by the old **shire counties**, like Lancashire or Kent. Below them were councils for **non-county boroughs** (large towns or cities with less than 50,000 inhabitants and sometimes known as *municipal boroughs*), **urban districts** (for towns) and **rural districts** (for country areas).

<u>Under the two-tier system the upper tier dealt with things like roads, police, planning and education, while the lower tier dealt with housing, social services and other more local needs.</u>

Outside the two-tier system were the large towns and cities which had single, or **unitary**, authorities known as **county boroughs**. In these, the one council provided all services. There was a separate system for London which had a two-tier structure of **London County Council** and **Metropolitan Boroughs**.

- 47 **Shire Counties** remained in England and Wales, although some of the old ones were abolished or merged (e.g. Rutland abolished and Herefordshire merged with Worcestershire) and some new ones were created (Avon, Cleveland and Humberside). Below them were **District Councils**.

- In heavily built-up areas, where several towns and cities have run together (e.g. Greater Manchester or West Midlands) **Metropolitan Counties** were formed, with **Metropolitan Districts** or **Boroughs** in the lower tier.

- In London there was the **Greater London Council** with 32 **London Boroughs** in the lower tier.

- Scotland had **Regions** (e.g. Borders or Strathclyde) instead of counties.

During the 1980s the Metropolitan Counties and Greater London Council were abolished, leaving the Metropolitan and London Boroughs as **unitary authorities**.

In the latest round of reforms that began in the 1990s, the national government decided that it wanted councils to become **enablers**. This means that, instead of offering services themselves, **councils buy services** from firms or groups who tender for the contracts. To help matters, the government also wanted to make all councils into single tier, or unitary, authorities. This was an easy matter in Wales and Scotland where the Welsh and Scottish Offices made the decisions and imposed a pattern of unitary bodies. But in England it was decided to respect the wishes of the electorate and a **Local**

Government Commission under **Sir John Banham** was set up to ask the public's opinion.

That public opinion saw to it that the most unpopular measures introduced in 1974 were reversed. Old counties like Rutland were reintroduced, while Avon, Cleveland and Humberside were abolished. But taking the wishes of the public into consideration meant that there is still no general agreement on a uniform pattern of unitary authorities and the country remains divided into a mixture of unitary and two-tier authorities. Typical of the confusion is the case of Hereford and Worcester where the two former counties were once more divided but, whereas Worcestershire returned to being a shire county with a second tier of district councils, Hereford also became a county council but in the form of a single unitary body.

Local Government - Councillors and Officials

For local elections, counties are divided into **divisions** and districts into **wards**. In county council elections the whole council is elected every four years. District councillors are elected for four years as well, sometimes with the whole council being re-elected, *but in most councils one third of the council stands down and is re-elected in turn,* this taking place in each of the three years when there is not a county council election.

Except for Northern Ireland local elections have always been held according to the first-past-the-post system but one of the measures proposed by the Liberal Democrats in return for their support for a Labour executive in the Scottish Parliament was the introduction of proportional representation for Scottish local elections.

Like candidates for parliament, anyone over the age of 21 who is on the electoral register can stand for local election, <u>but they must live or work in the area of the council on which they want to serve</u>. Candidates for the council <u>cannot be employed by the council,</u> so a teacher could not be a councillor in the area of the local education authority which employed that teacher. Unlike parliamentary elections, however, members of the House of Lords or citizens of another European Union country can stand for the local council of the area where they live.

Councillors are not paid, although they do get expenses and an attendance allowance for any council work they do. Because they are unpaid, but have to do a great deal of work, councillors tend to be people who are self-employed or retired.

The whole council meets regularly but not too often. Except for general policy decisions like fixing the council tax rate there are not many major policy decisions that are taken by the council as a whole. <u>Most of the council's work is done in committees,</u> with the committees referring their decisions to the council meeting for final approval. Most council work is concerned with running services, with decisions needing to be taken continually about their operation: the whole council could not spare the time for day-to-day decisions and it is also far too big a body to reach such decisions quickly.

Each service provided by the council has its own committee - **education committee, housing committee, highways committee, social services committee** and so on. There is also a co-ordinating policy committee, usually known as the **Finance and General Purposes Committee**. All these

129

committees are divided into sub-committees to deal with specialised interests. It has been said that policy decisions are really made in sub-committees, rubber-stamped by the committee and then rubber-stamped again by the council as a whole. This could be important if it were true because the public is allowed into council and committee meetings, *but not* into sub-committee meetings.

Committees are run by the **committee chair** and **vice-chair**, assisted by the relevant **chief officer** and **deputy chief officer**. At the head of the whole council the elected **Leader** works closely with the head of the council's officers. known as the **Chief Executive**. Chairs of the council and the various committees, as well as its leader, are chosen from the majority party on the council. Where, as is often the case today, there is no overall control, two or more parties will agree to share the chairs between themselves.

Local government officers are full-time, permanent, paid employees of the council; they are like a local civil service. Like civil servants they are supposed to be **neutral** and serve without favour whichever party is in power. But, unlike civil servants, council officials are usually professionally trained experts in their field - education officers will often be former teachers, the chief highways officer will be a civil engineer and so on.

Council officers:

- carry out the council's policies through finding out how they will work.

- provide the information needed to form council policy.

- provide expert advice in their professional capacity.

Local Government Finance

Local government gets its money from four possible sources:

- About **60%** comes from **government grants**.

- About **30%** comes from **local taxation**.

- About **10%** comes from **revenue in fees and charges**.

- <u>Large scale capital expenditure</u>, such as building houses or new schools, can be financed by **borrowing**, although there are strict rules laid down by central government as to how much may be borrowed and for what purpose.

<u>Government grants are of two types:</u>

Specific grants are large sums of money paid to local councils by the central government in order to pay for services that are provided by the councils because they are required to do so by the government. <u>These grants are to pay for specific services and must not be used for anything else.</u>

Block grants include the **Revenue Support Grant** and represent the amount given to local authorities by central government without directions as to its use. Councils get different amounts depending on the standard of living in the areas concerned, because the block grant is one way in which the poorer regions of the country can be given more money at the expense of the more affluent regions, through what is known as the **Standard Spending Assessment**, under which it is decided <u>how much money each council in the country requires to provide a level of service that is standard for the whole country</u>. In recent years the block grant has been used by central government to control local government because <u>the</u>

government can cut the size of the grant if it believes that a council has been over-spending beyond government guidelines.

Local taxation takes two forms:

A tax on businesses.

This was once part of the system of rates paid to the local district council, but responsibility for fixing the rate and its collection has now been taken out of the hands of the local authorities. The **Standard Business Rate** is fixed and collected nationally and then re-distributed to the councils according to the Standard Spending Assessment.

A tax on domestic housing.

Until 1990 this was done through the rates, which were calculated on the basis of what the value of a house would be if it were rented. The system was much criticised for being unfair, complicated and inefficient.

After years of argument the rates were replaced by the **community charge** - or **poll tax**, as it was better known. This meant that each individual in a local authority district had to pay the same amount of tax, no matter how rich or poor they were. It was seen as even more unfair than the rates and was wildly unpopular.

After two years of massive protest the poll tax was replaced by the **council tax** which is based on the value of a house if it were sold, payment being for the household and not the individual and with rebates for the less well off and those people living alone.

Trading revenue:

This is an unimportant part of council income - less than ten per cent, and even less in some cases - but it is quite significant and affects most residents of an area at one time or another. There are many ways in which councils can make charges, and this category covers - charging fines for overdue library books; entrance fees for the local swimming baths, golf course or sports centre; hiring out council buildings and providing catering for public functions; fares on council owned transport etc., etc. Council house rents are, of course, a form of revenue but these have to be paid into a special housing account and cannot be used as general revenue.

Changes in Local Government

Changes in the provision of services are very noticeable in local government. because the Conservative governments of the 1980s and early 1990s disliked local government -

- partly because they blamed local authorities for being the biggest spenders of public money

- partly because many local councils, especially in the big cities, were Labour controlled.

The Conservative governments of the 1980s reduced the powers of local government. The late Nicholas Ridley, a former minister, said that the ideal form of local government was a body that met once a year in order to hand out contracts for the provision of services. As a result successive government legislation was introduced with the intention of changing councils into **"enabling bodies"**. The consequence has been that councils which used to provide their own services through their own work-force have been required to allow private firms to bid to provide public services through **compulsory competitive tendering**. After the *'winter of discontent'* in 1979 it was believed that **local council direct labour** was <u>inefficient, over-manned, uneconomic and dominated by the trade unions</u>. Allowing private firms to provide services is to improve efficiency through competition, cutting down costs and removing out-dated practices. Nothing prevents the council's own workers from providing these services but they must tender for the contract, knowing that the contract will go to the lowest tender. Known since 1988 as **market testing**, competitive tendering is now applicable to most local government services, including:

- <u>Refuse collection and cleansing</u>: covering all cleaning services from emptying dustbins and recycling waste to sweeping the streets and clearing up litter.

- <u>Catering</u>: meaning not only providing school meals and meals for welfare and social services, but also council staff canteens, refreshments in leisure centres, council functions etc.

- <u>Parks and gardens</u>: which also takes in the management and maintenance of sports grounds, golf courses, swimming pools etc.

- <u>Vehicle pool repair and maintenance</u>.

Transfer to national control

At the same time as services were being contracted out to private firms, many bodies formerly controlled by elected local authorities were forced or encouraged to opt out of local authority control to be run by quangos or agencies <u>directly appointed, financed and controlled by national government:</u>

- Opted out grant maintained schools (GMS) and colleges.

- Health authorities, trust hospitals, family health services.

- Training and education councils (TECs).

- Urban development corporations.

- Housing action trusts.

These were mostly ideas produced by the Thatcher and Major Conservative governments but the New Labour government of Tony Blair may not have extended the process but it did not reverse it.

Changes to the structure of local government

One important constitutional change introduced by the Blair government was the proposed new structure of government for London which would include an **elected mayor** as city boss, on the European or United States model, supported by a small, elected **strategic body**. This Mayor would speak up for the interests of London, and be responsible for economic planning, transport, economic development, environmental issues, the police, fire service, land-use, cultural affairs and strategic planning etc. The mayor would also head a small, strategic assembly of 24 to 32 members, elected by a majority voting system.

An alternative to the proposed London system is that, subject to referendum, local councils should replace the existing committee system with an elected mayor and a form of cabinet government such as, for example, has been put into place by the London borough of Hammersmith & Fulham. In this system an elected executive mayor has extensive powers. Committee chairmen, now running services like education and housing, would be replaced by "local ministers" each with executive powers and forming a "cabinet" known as the 'mayor's board', whose actions could be referred to a 'scrutiny committee' and questioned by any councillor.

Revision exercise 9:

How much do you know about your own local government?

Do you live in a unitary authority or are there two-tiers?

Do you know the name or names of the councillor or councillors for the ward(s) in which you live - and what party or parties do they belong to?

Which party controls your local council or is there no overall control?

CHAPTER NINE

Europe

The European Communities

The European Communities were formed by the **Treaty of Rome** in **1957**. There were three communities originally:

European Coal and Steel Community (ECSC)

European Atomic Energy Communityty (Euratom)

European Economic Community (EEC)

It was the EEC, intended to be an economic grouping big enough to challenge the USA, and known as **the Common Market**, that was the most important. In 1967 the three communities merged to form **the European Community (EC)**. The next major change came in 1988 when all members of the EC signed the **Single European Act**, according to which trade barriers and customs duties between member countries were removed and a **Single Market** created. In 1992 came the **Treaty of Maastricht**, which created the **European Union (EU)**, extending the EC to include cooperation in defence, security and foreign affairs. Maastricht also confirmed the Single Market, gave citizens of all member countries full citizenship of the EU, promised social legislation and agreed on future political and economic union, from which Britain secured certain opt-outs from the monetary and security aspects of the Maastricht Treaty, opt-outs confirmed in the **Amsterdam Agreement** of 1997.

<u>The European Community has grown:</u>

- **France, Germany, Italy, Belgium, Luxembourg** and the **Netherlands** signed the Treaty of Rome in 1957. They were known as **'The Six'.**

- **Denmark**, the **Republic of Ireland** and the **United Kingdom** joined in 1972.

- **Greece** joined in 1981.

- **Spain** and **Portugal** joined in 1986.

- **Austria, Finland** and **Sweden** joined in 1995.

<u>Norway twice applied for membership and was accepted (in 1972 and 1995) but each time the people of Norway voted against membership in a referendum.</u>

In line for membership in 2002 are Poland, Hungary, Slovakia, the Czech Republic and Cyprus.

At the head of the European Union, making policy decisions and issuing directives like a government of the EU, is the **Council of Ministers**, which is made up of one minister from each member country. Usually, for routine business, the minister concerned is the Foreign Minister. But <u>when special issues are being discussed, the minister who attends is the minister concerned with that special issue, e.g. when agriculture is discussed, it is the Agriculture Ministers for the 15 countries who form the council</u>. Each member country in turn acts as **President of the EC** for six months (Jan-June and July-Dec.). During those six months all Council of Ministers meetings are chaired by the relevant minister from the country holding the presidency.

At least once every six months there is a **"summit meeting"** attended by the prime ministers of all member countries (for France the meetings are attended by the President). These are known as **European Councils** and they are held in the country holding the presidency at that time (for example, the Treaty of Maastricht was agreed at a European Council meeting when the Netherlands held the presidency). European Councils only last for a day and a half but they are useful meetings for reviewing general policy and, since they are usually held at the end of the six months, they can be used to summarise progress during the presidency just ending. European Councils can also appoint and receive reports from **Intergovernmental Commissions (IGCs)** which are special committees set up to examine major changes to the EU such as the Single Market. An IGC to review Maastricht started in 1996 and reported at Amsterdam in 1997.

[Note that the European Council is not to be confused with the Council of Europe, which is a debating chamber set up in 1948 and nothing to do with the EU]

Institutions of the European Community

Apart from the Council of Ministers there are three major institutions of the European Community - the **Commission**, the **European Court of Justice** and the **European Parliament**.

The Commission:

Is the executive of the EC, not only providing the bureaucracy of the EC like civil servants but able to make policy decisions like government ministers. There are twenty commissioners representing all 15 member countries - Britain, France, Germany, Italy and Spain having two commissioners each and the rest one each. The Commission is appointed for five years, commissioners being nominated by their country.

Once appointed, a commissioner is expected to adopt a European attitude and not favour their country of origin. Each commissioner is given a portfolio to look after, like a government minister; e.g. Neil Kinnock is the Transport Commissioner. At the head of the Commission is the **President**, appointed by the European Council with the consent of the European Parliament. The President coordinates the work of commissioners and assigns their portfolios. He also acts as head of government for the EC, attending European Council meetings and representing the EU at international meetings.

The Commission has a staff of 15,000, 3,000 of which are employed in translating documents into the many official languages of the community. Staff are divided into **Directorates-General** which have policy responsibilities like government ministries.

The European Court of Justice:

Based in Luxembourg, the Court of Justice rules on community law as it is laid down in the various treaties setting up the component communities of the European Union. It can rule on disputes between member states, arbitrate between the Commission and member states and also over-rule national law where that conflicts with community law. The court is made up of one judge for each member state. Most cases are heard before a panel of three judges, or five judges for more complicated issues.

(The European Court of Justice must not be confused with the European Court of Human Rights, which is part of the Council of Europe.)

The European Parliament:

Originally an assembly of nominated delegates the **EP** became a directly-elected parliament in 1979. There are now **626 members**, with the numbers for each country decided by its size; from the smallest, Luxembourg, with six MEPs, to the largest, Germany, with 99 MEPs (the UK has 87). With **Assembly Chambers** in Strasbourg and Brussels, the EP spends one week in every month in full plenary sessions, with debates, question time and reports from commissioners. The important work is done in one of 20 standing committees, based in Brussels, which take up two weeks of every month. The committees work with the Commission in drafting legislation and working up amendments to legislation, about a third of which become community law. The powers of the EP are:

- To vote on the acceptance of new member states.

- To reject or amend Council decisions affecting the Single Market.

- To reject or amend the EC Budget.

- To dismiss the entire Commission, on a two-thirds majority.

- To accept or reject a new President of the Commission.

MEPs work within European party groups of which the two largest are the **Party of European Socialists (PES)** on the left (with the British Labour Party as the largest national party in the PES) and the **European People's Party** on the centre-right (this is largely made up of Christian Democrats and although the Conservative Party is allied to the EPP they have tried to keep a distance between them because the EPP is as strongly in favour of European unity as the Conservatives are opposed to it).

The EP appoints an **ombudsman** to look into maladministration.

Appealing to Europe

In the past few years increasing numbers of people have found that political action can be taken in Europe when it is blocked in this country. This is particularly true of legal action taken in the courts, and with an increased number of pressure groups that find it easier to operate in Europe than it is in Britain.

The Courts:

There are two Courts in Europe which are open to British citizens when they have failed to get satisfaction from the British courts, including the House of Lords. These courts are-

1 **The European Court of Human Rights**, based in Strasbourg, and part of the **Council of Europe**. The court exists to enforce the <u>European Convention for the Protection of Human Rights and Fundamental Freedoms</u>, which Britain signed in 1950. The court is open to anyone who feels that they have been refused their basic human rights in their own country. The importance of this court for Britain is likely to diminish since one of the early acts of the Blair government was to recognise the European Convention as applying to the UK and anyone wishing to seek protection through the Convention can now do so through the British courts, without needing to go to Strasbourg.

2 - **The European Court of Justice**, based in Luxembourg, is one of the institutions of the **European Community**. The court is open to anyone who feels that they are being denied rights which they should have as EU citizens.

There have been successful appeals by British citizens <u>to both courts</u> involving such things as <u>the rights of pregnant women to serve in the armed forces; the right to belong or not belong to a trade union; the unfairness of pensions being</u>

143

paid at different ages for men and women; the rights of part-time workers, and so on.

Pressure and interest groups:

In recent years many pressure and interest groups have found it more worthwhile working in Brussels, finding it far easier to gain access to members of the European Commission than it is to attract the attention of British politicians and civil servants. The sort of interest groups involved are of various types:

Regional groups and local authorities. Some groups have offices in Brussels that are almost like embassies for the regions concerned. Some British regions, such as Wales, have an office in Europe to promote the region to European industries looking to set up new offices and factories. Some local authorities also approach the Commission directly. Liverpool, for example, sent several delegations to Brussels, *ignoring the British government,* so as to get EC funds for Merseyside.

National interest groups. These groups find that it is worth having some representatives in Europe. Contact with the European Parliament and Commission is particularly important for groups who are not well received by the present British government - such as trade unions and groups working for the interests of women, consumers or the environment.

Euro-groups. These are interest groups that are represented in several, if not all, the member states of the European Community. The most important Euro-groups are organisations which represent a particular area of interest. Typical examples are the **European Trade Union Confederation (ETUC)** and the **European Bureau of Consumer Organisations (BEUC)**.

International pressure groups with cross-European organisations: These are groups like **Green Peace** who have organisations in all member countries, but who coordinate their actions if several countries of the EU are involved. For example, the campaign against Shell Oil in 1995, <u>to prevent the dumping of an oil-rig, was carried out by Green Peace in Britain, Germany, the Netherlands and other EU countries, all acting together</u>.

The Single Market

When the European Community was set up in the 1950s, part of it was known as the **Common Market**. The idea was that by joining European countries together industry would have a <u>home market as big as the United States</u>. If there was free trade between members of the Common Market, <u>without having to pay customs duty and fill in forms every time a border was crossed</u>, then trade would get better and cheaper, while members of the Common Market would get richer.

Moves to turn the <u> Common Market into *a true single market,*</u> with no border restrictions between member countries, only really began in the 1980s. Once it began, however, everything moved very quickly. The **Single European Act** setting up the **Single Market** was signed in 1987 and came into force on 1 January 1993.

The Single Market is based on four freedoms:

- **Freedom of movement for goods** - goods manufactured in one member country can be sent to another member country without paying customs duties, and with a minimum of paperwork and delay at border crossings. In Britain that is best seen in the numbers of people crossing the Channel so as to bring back beer and wine on which they do not have to pay duty.

- **Freedom of movement for people** - citizens of any member country also become citizens of the EU and are free to travel, live and work anywhere in the EU. For tourists it means passport-free trips to France and Spain.

- **Freedom of movement for capital** - means that businesses in one member country are free to invest and set up branches in any other member country. French companies own shares in British water companies, while British investors have put money into French insurance companies.

- **Freedom of movement for services** - citizens of the EU have freedom to look wherever they want for services like banking or insurance.

The British government under Mrs Thatcher was very keen on the Single Market because it introduced **market forces** to trade in Europe. An important part of the Single European Act was to strengthen **competition policy**.

- **Policy on monopoly** - firms which dominate a market, and which can therefore charge anything they like, are not allowed to use their monopoly of the market to over-charge consumers.

- **Anti-cartel policy** - companies are not allowed to form **'cartels'**, in which a number of firms get together to fix prices in their favour. A typical example is the policy on air fares, where the national airlines of Europe have got together to fix a high rate for common fares on routes between European cities. EU policy is to stop this.

- **Policy on state aid** - some governments give money to private companies. The EC is careful to note the difference between state money given to help a company in difficulty, and money given to a company to help it undercut competitors from other countries.

The obvious next step after the **Single European Act**, and the **Treaty for European Union** (the Maastricht Treaty) which followed it, is that Europe should move on to **political and monetary union**. But Britain has an opt-out clause from the Maastricht Treaty which means that Britain did not need to join the European Monetary System when it began in January 1999.

The Issue of Europe

The issue over Europe is not so much whether Britain should be a member of the European Union or not. Most people are agreed that Britain should be a member but there is disagreement over the form the European Union should take, and over the nature of British membership.

There are the **federalists** who believe in a **supranational** Europe: in other words they believe that the countries of the EU should come together as one federal country - a United States of Europe. These are the **euro-enthusiasts** and include the Liberal Democrats, most of the Labour Party and some of the left wing of the Conservative Party.

There are the **functionalists** who believe in an **intergovernmental** Europe: who are members of Europe for what they can get out of it and see Europe as largely an association of independent nation states who get together for the benefit of trade and industry. These are the **euro-sceptics** who believe that Britain as a country must not be dictated to by Brussels. The euro-sceptics form a large and important part of the Conservative Party, but also a small but significant part of the Labour Party.

There are certain European issues over which the euro-sceptics feel very strongly:

- **Monetary union** - the **Treaty of Maastricht** agreed to unite the economies of member countries, with a **common currency** and a **European Central Bank**. Euro-sceptics believe that monetary union would mean that a British Chancellor could no longer control British tax and interest rates. They are also opposed to *'giving up the pound'*. In the Maastricht Treaty John Major won an **opt-out** for Britain which means that this country can choose whether or not to join the monetary union if and when it happens. The position stressed by Tony Blair and Gordon Brown is that Britain will join the monetary union and the single currency **when and if** it suits British interests to do so. They have also pledged that

148

Britain will only join the single currency with the approval of the British people <u>as shown in a referendum</u>. They agree that such a referendum is unlikely before the next election.

- **The Social Chapter** - the Maastricht Treaty includes many **social policies** like <u>a minimum wage, equal rights for women workers and safeguards for part-time workers</u>. The Conservative government of the time claimed that the cost to employers would make British firms uncompetitive, and <u>John Major got a British opt-out on social policies as well</u>. The Labour Party, however, were very much in favour, since it was the social policies of the EU that turned the Labour Party under Neil Kinnock into becoming pro-European instead of anti-European. At the time of their 1997 election victory, the Labour government accepted the Social Chapter in principle and since then most aspects have been accepted by the British government, including the granting of a statutory minimum wage.

- **The National Veto** - normally the decisions made by the **Council of Ministers** have to be unanimous, with all member states agreeing. <u>Just one country can block any decisions approved by the other 14 members</u>. In the early days of the Common Market, the French bias in the **Common Agricultural Policy** was created by the French President, Charles De Gaulle, refusing to agree with anything that did not suit French farmers. There are those who want to replace this with a form of **majority voting**, which is seen as <u>fairer and more democratic</u>. The euro-sceptics disagree because they believe that <u>the right of a British minister to block the wishes of the other member countries is the last defence</u>

of British rights. In 1996 the British government used its veto to block any decision making in Europe as part of its strategy to force Europe to abandon its ban on British beef.

- **Common security** - in what is known as the **'Schengen Agreement'** the EU wants to do away with border checks between member states. The eurosceptics in Britain object because they think that removing passport and customs checks at the border will encourage the activities of terrorists, drug smugglers and illegal immigrants. The British and Irish governments negotiated opt-out clauses from Schengen, as did Denmark and Sweden.

Revision exercise 10:

The advantages and disadvantages of belonging to the EU make a good subject for a classroom discussion. Consider your own position carefully - in favour, against or just don't know. Prepare the arguments to defend your position but please do not rely on some of the silly, biased arguments put forward by the tabloid newspapers.

PART THREE

POLITICAL ISSUES

CHAPTER TEN

An Introduction to Political Issues

The word 'issues' is used a lot in politics.

- During election campaigns politicians tell one another to '*deal with the issues*', to '*stick to the issues*' and to deal in '*issues rather than personalities*', claiming that other politicians are '*unable to face the issues*'.

- These days, voting behaviour has become '*issue-related*' and electors are encouraged to choose between competing issues as if they were shoppers searching for the best bargains in Tesco. Voters choose the party they believe will deal best with those issues they see as being important.

What is meant by this term **political issues**? The political commentator, Dennis Kavanagh, says that important political issues have three things in common:

- They are things over which public opinion is sharply divided.

- They are things about which voters feel very strongly.

- They are things which voters expect political parties to solve.

These are the three characteristics by which a topic is measured if it is classed as an issue in this book.

We can divide issues into three main areas:

- Issues dealing with the way in which the country is run. Included under this heading are really important things such as:

  economic issues

  social and welfare issues

  law and order

  defence and foreign affairs.

These are issues which influence voting behaviour because they affect the daily life and standard of living of every citizen. It is therefore important to the hopes of voters that the best party to deal with these issues is in power.

- Issues dealing with the way the country is governed are called **constitutional issues**. Included are:

  electoral reform

  reform of the House of Lords

  the role of the Monarchy

  a Bill of Rights and a written constitution

  nationalism and devolution.

These issues are not so closely linked with the major political parties, they are more the concern of pressure groups and the minor political parties.

154

- Issues dealing with the way people live and are treated include such things as:

  the environment

  race relations

  women's rights.

These issues mostly affect pressure and interest groups, although the major parties may become involved if forced to do so by public opinion. For example, politicians of all parties were converted to 'green' policies by the success of the Green Party in the 1989 European elections.

How issues are created

All issues are not the same either in their importance or in the length of time they remain important to the public and politicians. Some issues are always there, although they are more important at some times than at others. Other, more temporary issues, suddenly appear out of nowhere, become very important for a time, and then fade away again.

What makes an issue and what keeps it going?

Many issues are created by political parties who want to publicise their own policies and talk down the policies of opposing parties. The message from the parties is backed up

- *by the media*
  - *by party publicity on billboards or in newspaper advertisements*

- *through interest groups like trade unions*

  - *by public relations work carried out by lobbying groups*

    - *or by the daily experiences of the electorate*

Through this constant exposure the electorate see that there are issues about which they need to make up their own minds. Most people support a political party and that support is partly determined by the party's attitude to issues concerning the electorate.

For issues where political parties are not involved, the issue usually begins with <u>a feeling that something is wrong or that something needs doing.</u> Environmental issues are typical of worries which have affected people in recent years and caused people, who before that had nothing to do with politics, to get involved. In recent years there has been a lot of pressure group activity, over things like the export of veal calves and the destruction of the environment to build motorways, that has involved all sorts of middle class people whom one would never have thought of as political activists.

Issues are kept alive by the media. The British press is very biased - 70% of it in favour of the Conservatives. And the newspapers make a point of pushing those news stories which show off their favourite party's policies. Or, more often, they will sensationalise stories that show the opposing party in a bad light.

Issues and political parties

Political parties have **aims, objectives, values** and **ideas** - ways of thinking which make up what is known as **the party's ideology**. It is the ideology of a party which decides its attitude towards political issues.

Very roughly speaking there are two different views of society - Liberty versus Equality.

Liberty means:

- the freedom of the individual from government interference

- defence of an individual's rights and property

- an economy based on market forces of supply and demand

- the need for competition

- keeping up a country's historic freedom and independence.

Equality means:

- that an individual must surrender some individual rights for the common good

- property should be shared on the grounds of fairness

- governments should intervene when market forces have failed

- the strong must help the weak

- injustices of the past must be put right

- co-operation for the common good, nationally and internationally.

These are the two positions which can be said to divide the political parties. The line between the two is not always clear-cut and party members can differ greatly. But, by and large, <u>it is the way the party thinks about liberty or equality which decides their attitude to issues</u>. The Conservative Party is very much in favour of the freedom of the individual, private enterprise and market forces. The Labour Party is traditionally about equality and the general good of society. The Liberals are in favour of the individual but with a social conscience.

In time, some issues become out-dated and a party's view of an issue can change a great deal. For example, when the constitution of the Labour Party was written in 1919 the party's commitment to public ownership was written into the party constitution as **Clause Four** but, with time, Clause Four became an embarrassment which had to be got rid of by New Labour under Tony Blair.

Serious differences over an issue are sometimes not between parties but inside a party, with the result that an issue can split and possibly destroy that party. This ability for an issue to split a party is shown today in the way the Conservative Party is so divided over Europe, as has already been shown in chapter nine. The Labour politician, Roy Hattersley, has pointed out that arguments in the Labour Party over the issues which lost them the election of 1979 - such as unilateral nuclear disarmament, the sale of council houses and the role of the unions, among other things - so

158

weakened and divided the party as to keep it out of office for 18 years.

CHAPTER ELEVEN

Economic Issues

Perhaps the most important issue by which voters in elections judge the various political parties, is <u>how well the parties manage the economy</u>. How it is managed decides for most people what is known as **'the feel-good factor'**. This assumes that there are certain things which people need to feel are alright, both for themselves and for their families.

<u>In order for people to feel good they need to feel that:</u>

- They have a <u>good, safe job</u>.

- <u>They are well paid</u>, and will continue to receive pay increases.

- <u>They can own their own home</u>, and their home is a good investment.

- They have a good <u>and improving</u> standard of living.

- <u>They do not pay too much in taxes</u>.

- The value of their pay and savings is <u>not harmed by high inflation</u>.

When it comes to choosing a party to vote for in a general election the main thing that the voter is concerned about is how well the various political parties can manage the economy so as to provide this <u>feel good factor</u>.

Traditionally the Conservative Party always did well on economic issues because it was felt that there was a basic competence in the way that Conservative governments handled the economy. That belief, however, was shattered on Black Wednesday in September 1992 when interest rates rose to an all-time high of 15% and the Chancellor, Norman Lamont, spent £5 billion supporting the pound's place in the *exchange rate mechanism.*

<u>In the past there were two different views on running the economy:</u>

- **The Socialist view** was that all trade and industry should be <u>publicly owned</u> and that the whole of the <u>economy should be planned and run by the government.</u>

- **The Capitalist view** was that all trade and industry should be <u>privately owned</u> and <u>the government should have nothing to do with the running of the economy</u>.

For many years, from about 1950 to 1979 the economy was run by a compromise between these two viewpoints, in what was known as **the post-war consensus**. Britain had a **mixed economy** that was a <u>mixture of private firms and nationalised industries</u>, and, while there was not a planned economy, the government did feel free to take a hand if trade or industry got into trouble. The consensus governments of the 1950s and 60s provided -

- nearly full employment.

  - very low inflation.

    - an improving standard of living.

162

The feel-good factor was so strong that the Conservatives won the 1959 election on the slogan *"You've never had it so good"*.

The years of consensus ended in the 1970s when there was:

<u>high inflation</u>

<u>poor growth in the economy</u>

<u>and rising unemployment.</u>

The Conservative Party, led by Margaret Thatcher, broke the consensus by saying that the government should not interfere in the running of the economy.

- nationalised industries should be **privatised**.

- companies should be run by **market forces** - <u>the laws of supply and demand</u>.

- there should be <u>no government help</u> for companies in trouble and <u>inefficient companies should be closed down</u>, even at the cost of high unemployment.

This view of the economy, known as **the market economy**, has been quite successful and is one of the reasons that the Conservatives were in power for so long after 1979. Even the Labour Party accepted the market economy and <u>got rid of its old socialist commitment to nationalised industries through</u> **Clause Four**. But the economy ran down in the late 1980s and <u>the Conservatives lost the feel-good factor</u>.

All parties may have become committed to a market economy but they do not necessarily think about it in the same way. There are two views of what is meant by a market economy:

- **A totally free market** without any restriction on the operation of companies except that they should work in the interests of the shareholders.

or

- **A market** which is free and competitive but which is **regulated** in some ways, so as to safeguard the interest of the public.

Taxation

Taxation exists to raise money for the government to spend, but it can have other uses:

- The **redistribution of wealth**, by which money is taken from those with a lot of money in order to provide services for those with far less money. This was first done in the so-called 'People's Budget' of 1909, when Lloyd George, the Chancellor of the Exchequer, needed to raise £16 million for the government's social programme, such as old age pensions, and he decided that the money should come from the rich. Since 1945 the Labour Party has taken over the idea first put forward by Lloyd George and, as a result, has become identified in the public's mind as the party of high taxation, not only because of Labour's spending policy but because taxation is seen as a way to make society more fair and equal.

- **Excise duties on tobacco, alcohol, petrol and betting** have for some time been known as '**taxes on sin**' and these taxes can be seen not only as raising money for the government but as <u>acting against anti-social behaviour</u>, whether it is encouraging people to give up cigarette-smoking or speeding up the change from leaded to unleaded petrol. The Green Party even suggests that income tax should be replaced by taxes to help the environment, such as road tolls, higher prices for air travel, noise level taxes on lorries, aircraft and motorcycles, taxes on waste and a tax on oil.

The issue of taxation centres on whether taxation is **direct** or **indirect**:

<u>Tax on what an individual earns</u> is known as **direct taxation**.

<u>Tax on what an individual spends</u> is known as **indirect taxation**.

- Direct tax like income tax is a **progressive tax**, which means that <u>the more you earn the more you pay.</u> This can be made even more progressive by increasing the rate at which income tax is paid as an individual earns more money. At the same time, a system of tax free allowances (money people are allowed to earn before they start to pay tax) helps to reduce the amount of tax taken from the low-paid.

- Indirect taxation is a tax on what the taxpayer spends and is, therefore, a **regressive tax**, <u>which does not consider a taxpayer's ability to pay.</u> If the VAT on an item in a shop is £2, then that £2 is far more important for

165

someone earning £60 a week than it would be for someone earning £200 a week. In the early days of VAT, there used to be different rates, so that <u>necessities were taxed at a lower rate than luxuries</u>. That has gone now, although certain necessities like food and children's clothing pay no VAT at all.

<u>Since 1980 there has been a slow change from direct to indirect taxation.</u>

- The Conservatives argue that <u>income tax stops people working hard</u> because the extra money they earn is taken away again in taxation. They also say that <u>income tax is not fair</u> because there is no choice as to whether to pay or not: income tax is enforced by law. On the other hand, a person can choose whether or not to spend money and <u>a tax on spending rather than on earnings allows an individual the freedom of choice.</u>

- Parties opposed to the Conservatives, however, argue that <u>indirect taxation is very unfair</u> because, when tax has to be paid on necessities such as clothes or transport or heating or light **there is no real choice** <u>as to whether the money has to be spent or not</u>. This move from direct to indirect taxation helps to explain why the Conservative government in the 1990s could claim to have cut taxes (<u>cuts in income tax</u>) while the Opposition claimed that taxes rose under the Conservatives (<u>increases in VAT and other indirect taxes</u>). In their own way both sides were right in what they said.

Taxation and Spending

The Conservative Party won the 1992 general election by promising to cut taxes while threatening that the Labour Party would have to raise taxes to pay for their heavy spending on things like the National Health Service. Since 1992 the Conservative government did cut the rate at which income tax is paid, as they promised. But more people on low incomes ended up paying income tax because the Conservatives did not increase personal tax allowances at the same rate. The Conservatives also increased **indirect or regressive taxation** which penalises the less well off and bears no relation to an individual's ability to pay.

The Conservatives have twice got into serious trouble over attempts to increase regressive taxes:

- **The poll tax**, when everyone was expected to pay the same amount of tax based on where they lived, no matter how much money they had or did not have.

- Raising **VAT on gas and electricity**, which was seen not only as a tax on necessities but, since children, the ill and old age pensioners are the ones in most need of heat and light, it was seen as a tax on those people least able to afford to pay it.

Both the poll tax and VAT on fuel show that, while people may put up with increases in indirect taxation if their income tax is cut, they will protest if that indirect taxation is seen to be unfair, especially if increases in indirect taxation are greater than reductions in direct taxation. The Conservatives argued that, while they did increase taxes, those tax increases

167

would have been much greater under Labour, because of the spending promises in Labour's manifesto. In suggesting this, they revealed the true issue over taxation, which is:

<u>Does the electorate want a high level of public services, paid for out of high taxation, or do they want low taxes, with a low level of public services as a result?</u>

This is very important as the **dependent population** increases. The term 'dependent population' means <u>the number of people in the country who do not, or cannot, work but are supported by those who do</u>, such as the unemployed, the chronically sick, young children, students or pensioners.

Everyone believes that if the electorate were able to choose between high and low taxation, they would always choose low taxation. However, there is an alternative known as **hypothecation**; a long and complicated word meaning <u>taxation raised for a special purpose</u>. For some years the Liberal Democrats have suggested raising the standard rate of income tax by one penny which would be just for spending on education. Strangely enough, the idea seemed to be quite popular with many people and did not lose the party any support. The suggestion seems to be that, while general tax increases without an obvious purpose might be resented, people would be more ready to pay higher taxes:

1   <u>if they knew what the money was to be spent on</u>

2   <u>if they approved of the service on which the money was to be spent.</u>

In an opinion poll carried out in April 1995, **60%** of those answering (including **52%** of Conservative voters) agreed that they would be willing to see the standard rate of income tax rise to 30p in the pound if the extra money were spent on services such as schools and hospitals. The issue of taxation is no longer an argument between **low taxes** and **high taxes** but about the difference between **fair taxes** and **unfair taxes**.

Unemployment

The Labour Party said for many years that it wanted to cut unemployment and return to full employment. But the term **'full employment'** does not mean 100% employment of the work force, because, at any one time there has to be a certain number who:

- have just left a job and have not yet got a new one.

- those who, for one reason or another, are unemployable.

To understand the difference between employment and unemployment, we must look at three different forms of unemployment:

1) **Temporary unemployment** is a pause between jobs, a break of anything from a few days to a few months, for a person who has finished one job and is waiting to start another. It includes **seasonal work** when workers who are taken on at a busy time are laid off at the end of the busy season.

2) **Cyclical unemployment** is created by the strength of the economy which goes in cycles. During a recession workers will be laid off because of a lack of demand. When there is

an economic recovery workers are taken on again.

3) **Structural unemployment** is the most serious because it is produced by changes in the nature of industry. The changes are permanent and once jobs are destroyed there is little chance of getting them back again. There are two main causes for this:

- The run-down of old out-dated industries; in which entire industries become less important or die, as has happened to coal-mining or ship-building. Or industries suffer from competition from elsewhere, as British textiles have suffered from cheap imports from India

- Technological change; in which human workers are replaced by machines. At first this affected manufacturing industry when machines replaced production line workers, but now it is affecting office-work like banking, where humans are being replaced by computers, electronic machines and the internet.

As well as the true unemployed there are many adults of working age who are not really employed and are known as **'economically inactive'**. They include:

- those who have taken early retirement

- the chronically ill or disabled

- those on training or re-training courses

- women who are classed as housewives

- single parents and others on social security.

They are not actually earning a wage and they often receive

social security payments, but <u>they are not part of the labour market</u>. In 1995, 19.8% of the workforce was in this group.

Will Hutton, a prominent political and economics journalist, divided the population into three groups according to how they fit into the country's pattern of employment and unemployment.

- 30% are **disadvantaged** - <u>they are out of work, or are economically inactive</u>.

- 30% are **insecure** - <u>they have work, but it is insecure, unprotected and without benefits like paid holidays</u>. They include part-time and casual workers as well as many of the self-employed and those on fixed-term contracts.

- 40% are **privileged** - <u>they have a full-time job or a part-time job that has lasted more than five years</u>.

<u>The issue of unemployment is no longer about being in or out of work, it is a question of</u>:

- <u>**which groups** of people are likely to be in work?</u>

- <u>**what kind** of work do they do?</u>

- <u>**what conditions** are attached to their employment?</u>

171

Changes in employment and unemployment

Over the whole 18-year period of Conservative government between 1979 and 1997, there were huge changes in the pattern of unemployment in Britain.

1979 - **1.25 million**

1980 - **2 million**

1982 - **2.67 million**

1986 - **3.4 million** - 14% of the working population.

1990 - **1.59 million** - 5.6%.

1993 - **2.99 million** - 10.6%.

1996 - **2.1 million**

More importantly, between 1979 and 1988 there were <u>no fewer than nineteen changes in the way government defines unemployment</u>. No longer counted as being really unemployed have been

- married women who leave work but do not claim benefit

- all those on schemes of training or re-training

- men aged over sixty or under eighteen

- anyone else who is 'not actively seeking employment'.

In 1995 a survey among adults of working age showed that:

- **19.8%** were **economically inactive**

- **1.1%** were on **government schemes** of one kind or another

- and **8.1%** were **unemployed...**

...placing 29% of the population <u>outside the active work force.</u>

<u>In the 1990s the whole structure of employment has changed:</u>

1) Figures from April 1995 showed that **35.9%** of the working population had **full-time** jobs, compared to a figure of **55.5%** in 1975: <u>a drop of 35% over twenty years.</u>

2) There was a slight increase in those calling themselves **self-employed**, from **5.5%** to **7.5%**, but in fact, very many more have <u>moved from full-time jobs into working part-time or</u> <u>on temporary short-term contracts.</u>

3) More and more men in their fifties are leaving the labour market through **early retirement**.

4) The length of time a person spends in a job is also less, <u>the average man's job lasting **six and a half years** and the average woman's just over **four**.</u>

<u>The old ideal of people leaving school and getting a job for life has gone for good </u>and the short-term, part-time nature of so much work, often without rights over things like sick pay, paid holidays and redundancy pay, <u>leads to a lack of security among even the employed.</u> Many people know that they may be in work at the moment but they do not know how long that will last before they too are out of work.

173

Another important thing is the role of women. 1995 represented a landmark because, in that year, <u>women were on the brink of taking over from men as more likely to be in work</u>; the figures for April 1995 showing that **49.4%** of all employees were women. Unemployment is increasingly something that concerns the men more than it worries the women:

<u>as against a national unemployment figure of 8.4%,</u>

<u>11.3% of the male working population were unemployed,</u>

<u>only 4.5% of women were unemployed.</u>

Pay

The changes in employment discussed above have helped to create **a low-wage economy** in Britain.

- Many new jobs in recent years have been jobs for women; <u>who traditionally are paid less, do not belong to trade unions and are very often part-time workers.</u>

- Many businesses have cut the pay of workers by saying that <u>without a cut in pay the firm would have to close</u>.

- Senior staff with high salaries have been encouraged to <u>take early retirement so as to make way for younger staff</u> who are paid much less.

- Workers in some firms have been sacked, <u>but then re-employed on a self-employed, freelance basis</u>; for less money and without benefits.

- Unlike the 1970s when the majority of workers expected

a pay rise every year, there were now workers who had not had a pay rise for two or even three years and who accepted the situation quietly for fear of unemployment.

The Conservative government opted out of the **Social Chapter of the Maastricht Treaty**, which required governments to legislate for **a minimum wage** and provide protection for part-time workers. A minimum wage for the British was attacked by government ministers because they claimed it would lose jobs, if employers could not afford to pay the wages. Multi-national companies began to move production to Britain from countries like France because British wage rates were lower than those in competing countries. Opposition politicians claimed that Britain was becoming known as *'the sweat-shop of Europe'*. Wages in Britain were even lower than they were in Korea or Malaysia.

After the Labour victory of 1997 hopes rose that a Labour government would introduce a minimum wage. This was indeed done but many people argued that the figure of £3.60, that was fixed on for the minimum hourly rate, remains an almost unacceptably low figure.

Low pay rates in the private sector were maintained through fear of unemployment and the declining power of the unions. A pay policy has largely been continued in the public sector through government policy that any rise in pay should be kept below the level of inflation. In 1995 the government approved a pay rise for teachers but refused to give local authorities the money to pay for the rise. For nurses, who had been awarded 3% rises, the government was only willing to contribute 1%, with the rest to be made up by local pay agreements.

In the mid-1990s the public began to show an increasing resentment at the huge pay increases being given to chief executives of the privatised utilities. One case which caused a considerable stir was that of Cedric Brown, former chief executive of British Gas, who was awarded a **75%** pay increase in 1995, taking his salary to **£475,000** a year. Other cases were Sir Desmond Pitcher, chairman of North West Water, whose salary had risen by **571%** since privatisation, and David Jeffries, chairman of the National Grid, paid an annual salary of **£359,000** and making a potential **£1.78 million** in share options.

The Conservative government of the time dismissed Opposition protests at these awards as *'the politics of envy'*, but this was not necessarily true. People may resent huge salaries being earned by just a few individuals but people mostly accept them as a fact of life.

<u>What does annoy the public is the unfairness in that:</u>

- these executives are being paid so much more than those who ran the utilities before they were privatised.

- they are being paid extremely large salaries when their workers are having to manage on far less; for example, <u>Cedric Brown's 75% increase was announced on the same day as 2,600 staff in British Gas showrooms faced 16% cuts in average salaries of £13,000 a year.</u>

- Much the same was true in July 1996 when MPs voted themselves a pay rise of 26%. What upset the voters was not so much that MPs did not deserve the money but that parliament was giving itself so big a pay rise at a time when the government was telling workers in the public

176

sector, like nurses and teachers, that they had to be satisfied with pay rises of 1 or 2 per cent.

Pay as a political issue is not about the amounts people earn but more about fairness - the motto of most people is "A fair day's work for a fair day's pay".

The Trade Unions

Trade Unions are not often seen as an important political issue now, because there were important changes in the 1980s that led to a massive drop in trade union power. To understand what has happened to the trade unions it is best to look back and see how the unions were widely criticised in the 1970s.

- Unions caused inflation by demanding huge wage increases every year.

- Union officials were old-fashioned stick-in-the-muds who prevented the introduction of new technology.

- Unions were responsible for poor productivity with their restrictive practices.

- Unions would not let managers manage.

The Conservative government of 1979 began a slow programme to remove many of the powers that had belonged to the unions - particularly the ability to call a strike without notice and the ability to use mass picketing to enforce a strike. It took nine separate pieces of legislation between 1979 and 1993 to bring in all the government's proposed reforms but when they were finished it meant that the trade unions could no longer do anything about government policy on pay, unemployment and privatisation.

As well as legislation, the government showed that it was willing to *"take on"* the unions in a series of show-piece strikes, of which the miners' strike of 1984-5 is the most famous. The government faced down the unions, showing that the government would not give way and were willing to sit out even the most damaging of strikes. And, a year after the miners' strike collapsed, News International, the newspaper group owned by Rupert Murdoch, sat out a similar damaging strike to ensure a union-free production plant for newspapers in Wapping, East London.

Other things apart from government action helped to reduce union power:

- Increasing unemployment was a double-edged weapon which both reduced the membership of trade unions and made the unions more reluctant to take industrial action. Between 1979 and 1993 union membership dropped from 13.3 million to 9 million.

- Unions were refused recognition, with 9 per cent of work places refusing to recognise unions that had previously had the right to negotiate in those places.

- Unions were offered recognition and sole representation in new plants, in return for **no-strike agreements**. This was particularly favoured by Japanese firms setting up assembly and manufacturing plants in Britain.

- Traditional industries with large work forces, which had once formed the top rank of the union movement, such as mining, iron and steel and ship-building, were in decline,

178

taking union influence and power with them.

- During the 1980s most new employment was shifting from the traditional heavy manufacturing industries to service industries like the retail trade, catering and financial services. <u>Service industries have a tradition of having a part-time, casual, largely female and non-unionised work force</u>.

- <u>Technological advances enabled unskilled, or differently-skilled, workers to do the work of previously powerful skilled tradesmen</u>, as for example, newspaper reporters who could type in their own stories to the computerised printers instead of needing hot-metal typesetters.

  - Whole industry collective bargaining was replaced by thousands of local, in-house agreements and deals. <u>The old ideal of workers getting together, for support and strength through numbers, was lost as the unions broke up</u>.

  - There was no major restoration of union rights and powers by the Blair government. Naturally a Labour government is more friendly towards the unions than the Conservatives ever were but New Labour is aware that the union connection lost them votes in the past and now are determined to maintain relations at a safe distance.

Privatisation

Privatisation takes various forms:

1 **Selling-off state-owned industries** in the name of efficiency and better service, by moving nationalised industries like British Gas from the public to the private sector, and therefore transferring ownership from the government to private shareholders.

2 **De-regulation** - the removal of government-made restrictions on enterprises like bus companies, in an attempt to allow free commercial competition.

3 **The contracting-out of services** previously provided by national or local government work-forces, like school meals, hospital cleaning or dustbin collection. These services are now provided by private firms who bid against one another for the contracts.

4 **Opening the public sector to market forces**. The provision of services has moved from civil service departments to government agencies. For example, the prisons are now run by the Prison Service Agency and not the Home Office.

The reason for privatising the nationalised industries was said to be so that competition would make them more efficient, but there were other, political, reasons:

- The government found that allowing anyone to buy shares in the privatised industries was very popular. Making money from privatisation created a new class of small shareholders who had never even thought of buying and selling shares before.

- Privatisation provided lots of money for the government. Revenue from the major privatisations ran into many billions of pounds in the mid eighties.

- Margaret Thatcher believed she had to reduce the power of the state: every industry privatised, and every service contracted out, was a further reduction in state power.

Privatisation has been criticised, not only by Labour:

- Waste of assets - not only the capital value of the companies but the loss of revenue from those public enterprises that made a profit.

- Against the national interest - privatisation could lead to the sale of important industries to foreigners. American, French and German companies have bought large shares in public utilities like electricity and water.

- Loss-making deals and sweeteners - public enterprises were often made 'suitable' for privatisation at great cost - by writing off debts for example - and then the companies were sold off for much less money than they were worth.

- Massive windfall profits - large sums of money were handed over to private shareholders thanks to shares in public utilities being undervalued when privatised. In one case, in August 1996, the management of Porterbrook, a train-leasing firm, sold their company to a private buyer for £825 million, just eight months after that management had bought the company off British Rail for £527 million - a profit of three hundred million pounds in eight months!

- <u>Public service or private profit?</u> - private investors may only be interested in the profitable sections of a public utility, parts that are not profitable will either be scrapped or replaced by an inferior service. For example, after bus de-regulation city streets were crowded with dozens of different buses, while many country areas had hardly any buses at all.

The Labour Party in opposition was against privatisation, and did everything it could to stop any new privatisations as they came along. But, as time went by, it became more and more difficult and more and more expensive to change what had been done already. Even when they came to power in 1997 Labour not only failed to re-nationalise British Telecom or British Gas but even began talking about what services - such as Air Traffic Control - they could themselves privatise. The only way in which Labour differed was in their willingness to accept a more stringent and searching regulatory code of practice for the privatised sector.

<u>The issue of privatisation has moved away from being one of 'for and against' to one of how much control the government keeps for itself. Labour now argues for a greater regulation of the services provided by the privatised companies and, above all, will argue for a high level of taxation on the vast profits made by the privatised utilities.</u>

CHAPTER TWELVE

Social Issues

Welfare

There is just one major point at issue about social welfare; whether we are talking about <u>the health service, old age pensions, education, unemployment benefit or social security</u>. And that point is:

Should welfare be **universal** - <u>available to everyone and anyone without restriction?</u>

<u>**or**</u>

Should it be **selective** - <u>given only to those individuals who can prove they are in need?</u>

<u>At the heart of that argument is the cost of welfare and the question of who is to pay for it.</u>

There are two main criticisms about the cost of a **universal Welfare State**:

- The universal provision of welfare has no place in a market economy because giving money to people as a right and not out of need is opposed to market forces.

- The old idea of the Welfare State as looking after people *"from the cradle to the grave"* does away with individual initiative, self-respect and healthy competition, creating a '**dependent society**'.

Most of today's problems with the Welfare State have come about because things were very different when the system was introduced in 1948.

i) The 1940s, 50s and 60s saw nearly full employment, with every one paying tax to pay for welfare services. In the 1990s, with the economy in recession and with the growth of unemployment, there were people who:-

a) no longer paid tax because they were unemployed

b) now received unemployment benefit and social security.

This represents a double drain on the tax system.

ii) In the 1940s no one could see how the people's **standard of living** would rise. What were thought of as luxuries in 1945 had become necessities by the end of the century. Welfare benefit is supposed to provide money for essentials such as food, housing and clothes. But what about a **quality of life** that goes beyond **subsistence level**?

The Welfare State was originally intended as a safety-net to prevent people falling into **absolute poverty**. It was never intended to guarantee everyone a comfortable life-style.

iii) A growing number of students in full-time education and a greater expectation of life for old people as a result of better health care, added to the number of people making demands on welfare while not working and paying tax themselves. For example, there are many of the old, disabled and chronically sick who are unable to work and therefore do not pay tax. Once these people would have died before they had received much benefit: today they are living far longer and have become a long-term charge on social security.

v) The **role of women** has changed dramatically since the start of the Welfare State in 1948. Those setting up the Welfare State assumed that, as had been the case in the past, the average woman would give up work when she got married and she would then be supported for the rest of her life by her husband. No one could foresee the place in society that would be filled by women, particularly single women. Nor could anyone see the number of divorces there would be by the end of the century, nor the proportion of couples living together outside marriage, nor the increase in the numbers of **unmarried mothers** and **single-parent families**.

vi) These changes in the status of women makes the point that welfare provision in Britain is based on the household rather than the individual. For welfare purposes, the **ideal family**, as far as the government is concerned, still consists of a married couple, and their 2.4 children, with only the husband and father working. To assess welfare benefit it was assumed that any income earned by any individual forms part of <u>a joint household income for the support of all family members</u>. No one thought to make provision for the many single-parent families, single households, same-sex partnerships or any other present-day variation.

<u>Things have changed so much since 1948 that it is a major issue as to whether Britain can continue to afford a universal welfare system based on the nuclear family.</u>

Social Security

Social security includes a number of **universal, flat-rate** benefits paid for through **National Insurance**, which insures the citizen against unemployment, sickness or retirement through unemployment benefit, sick pay and the old age pension. Apart from these <u>there is a safety net of assistance</u> for those whose earnings fall below a minimum level, this assistance being **means-tested** and therefore **selective** in its provision.

Today the social security system is in difficulties. Frank Field, the maverick Labour MP who was briefly a social security minister in the Blair government, once said, '*We live in a world where increasingly people work fewer years and yet live longer in retirement. There is simply no way in which the welfare bills can be cut and yet each and every one can have an adequate pension*'. As has been said about taxation -

<u>Does the electorate want a high level of public services, paid for out of high taxation, or do they want low taxes, with a low level of public services as a result?</u>

The issues surrounding social security concern the cost of welfare and how that cost might be met.

There are a number of things that might be done about the cost of social security:

1) **Do nothing**, but allow the demands made on social security to rise, with a rise in taxes to pay for it as a result. This is not a serious possibility because no political party would dare suggest that taxes should be increased.

2) **Cut welfare benefits**. Again, this would not be popular with the voters. Many benefits, like the old age pension, are paid in return for contributions made over many years. It would probably be illegal to refuse a pension to people who had paid into the scheme all their working lives. The only option here is to cut back on benefits to persons who can be described as '**undeserving**', like unmarried mothers.

3) **Dismantle the Welfare State** and the social security system for all but the very needy. This is the solution put forward by the Tory Right. The '**No Turning Back**' Group of Thatcherite MPs proposed that **child benefit** should be scrapped, along with **state pensions** for those already possessing a pension from their job.

4) **Reduce the number of benefits given as of right** and **increase the number of benefits that are selective**. For example, after a given period, someone on unemployment benefit might only receive benefit if they agreed to a course of training or re-training. This was suggested by Gordon Brown as a possible policy for the Labour Party and resulted after 1997 in a re-definition of unemployment benefit as a '**job-seekers allowance**'.

187

5) **Transfer support from the family to the individual**. In Australia the social security system has moved away from the family unit. Instead of the household receiving income support, each unemployed partner is paid a separate benefit - unemployment benefit if seeking work or parenting benefit if looking after children. If one partner obtains work their benefit is reduced but the partner's benefit is not touched. This solves the **'why work?'** issue.

Social Security has changed in the 1990s. The British people tend to believe that spending on social security is too high and out of control. In fact, growth in social spending is quite modest compared with other industrialised countries, ranking at about eighteenth in the world order, when considered as a share of national income. Only Portugal in Western Europe spends less on welfare provision than Britain, while the Benelux and Scandinavian countries spend a third as much again.

The question of spending on the Welfare State is only a political issue if the politicians believe that low taxes are a priority.

Poverty

There is a difference between **absolute** poverty and **relative** poverty.

- **Absolute poverty** means not having enough money to maintain an acceptable quality of life in terms of food and shelter.

- **Relative poverty** simply means being poor compared with other people. <u>In a fairly rich country like Britain, the poor have a standard of living that would seem to be comfortable in a Third World country</u>.

The amount of money needed to provide a minimum standard of living is known as the **subsistence level**, and provides a **poverty line** beneath which someone lapses into absolute poverty.

When the Welfare State was set up in the 1940s it was intended that <u>unemployment or sickness benefit should be set at subsistence level so that everyone would have the **minimum essential** provision</u>. Unfortunately, those setting up the system were afraid of the cost and the benefits fixed in 1948 were only 70% of what was thought of as subsistence level. Because of this, far more people than was originally intended needed some sort of means-tested Income Support beyond the basic social security payments.

Because of this faulty calculation, the Welfare State, which was supposed to end poverty for ever, failed to do so. As early as 1960 it was found that although less than 5% of the population were actually living on or below the poverty line, 14% - 7.5 million - were living in relative poverty. Significantly large numbers of those living in poverty were children, and a high proportion of these were living in families where the father was working, but earning less than he would have received in benefit if he were out of work.

Family poverty has not improved since the 1960s, in fact one third of all families were receiving social security payments by 1995. Poverty has become a major political issue that helped to create pressure groups like the **Child Poverty**

Action Group and **Shelter**. It also created what is known as the **'Why Work?' issue**, as it became evident that many individuals, <u>and particularly single parents</u>, were caught in <u>a trap where any efforts to break out of poverty often had the effect of making people even poorer</u>. This was shown as long ago as 1971, when **Family Income Support (FIS)** was introduced. FIS was intended to be a <u>mean-tested benefit</u> for all families on low incomes, which would top-up earnings until they reached a reasonable level of income.

<u>The problem with FIS, which is typical of the **poverty trap**, was</u>:

- if recipients of FIS got a rise or a better-paid job, <u>the sum of 50p was deducted from FIS for every extra pound earned</u>.

- yet, as income increased, <u>the worker</u>, while still receiving FIS, <u>could start paying income tax and increased national insurance contributions, and families could lose out on relief payments like rent rebates or free school meals</u>.

As people said, *"If you can get more money by not working, why work?"* And, as the Labour MP, Frank Field, said, *"It is now a fact that for millions of low paid workers very large pay increases have the ridiculous effect of increasing a family's take home pay by only a little bit and in some cases a wage rise can actually make the family worse off."*

Education

Arguments about education have concentrated on two issues:

- A choice between **equality of opportunity** through open-entry comprehensive schools, or **selection by ability** through creaming off the more able into grammar schools.

- Concern as to what were seen as **falling standards** of education.

During the years of Conservative government the two issues became mixed together because the government believed that standards were falling because comprehensive schools had failed.

Kenneth Baker became Secretary of State for Education in 1986 and began to prepare what was known as the **GERBIL** (Great Educational Reform Bill). Baker made five points:

1) **Technical education** must be improved.

2) There should be a **National Curriculum** which would be tested regularly.

3) There should be <u>local management of schools</u> **opted out** <u>of local authority control</u>.

4) Schools would be ruled by **market forces** <u>because there would be parental choice</u>.

5) **To help parents choose** between good and bad schools, **performance league tables** would be published.

Typical of the suggested new schools were the **City Technical Colleges (CTCs)**, paid for by the government but sponsored by big business. Other schools were encouraged to opt out of local control to become **grant-maintained schools**, receiving rather more money from central government than local education authorities were given to run those schools still in their control.They were <u>independent schools run by educational trusts rather than local education authorities</u> and they were typical of the kind of schools the Conservative Party wanted:

- <u>Paid for by the government</u>, the amount decided by the number of students.

- <u>Full control of their own money.</u>

- <u>With a curriculum decided for them</u> by the Department of Education.

- <u>Powers transferred from local education authorities to parents, governors and the schools themselves.</u>

Similar moves were made for **colleges of further education** and those **polytechnics** which became full universities in their own right.

Baker's plans did not go exactly as he wished:

- The wide-ranging National Curriculum of ten compulsory subjects was simplified so much and so often that <u>it almost disappeared.</u>

- Instead of the original 20 CTCs proposed, <u>only 15 were set up at first.</u>

- Despite being given large sums of money, very few schools voted to opt out and <u>after five years only 1000 schools, or 5% of the total, had chosen to become grant-maintained</u>.

Critics of the government's policy point out the problems as:

1) Competition between schools drives parents, their children and the money towards the successful schools, but deprives the less successful of money and makes the bad worse.

2) Successful schools can choose their pupils on the grounds of ability, possibly through an entrance examination, bringing back the problems of selective education.

3) Although the reforms were introduced to help parents, and to allow a school to manage its own affairs, there is now a strong centralised control of education, at the expense of the local independence of schools, councils or parents.

Education - the political view

All parties agree that there are faults in the education system but there are deep disagreements as to the causes of those faults.

The Conservative viewpoint is that teachers and local education authorities have failed the schools because:

- <u>Comprehensive schools are too big</u> and treat children as if they were all the same.

- <u>Mixed ability teaching moves</u> at the pace of the slowest and <u>does not stretch the more able students</u>.

- There is <u>a failure of discipline in schools</u> and too many students get away with <u>disruptive behaviour</u> which disturbs the other students in the school.

- <u>Teachers in schools have too much freedom to choose what they teach</u> and how they teach it, often against the wishes of parents.

- There are too many <u>bad teachers who cannot be sacked</u>.

- There is <u>too little attention paid to English and Maths</u>, which mean that too many children leave schools without basic skills.

- There is <u>too much experimentation</u>, for example, with things like studying Coronation Street instead of Shakespeare, reducing the quality of education.

- Local councils, as the **local education authorities**, <u>have too much freedom</u> to decide on the nature of education in their areas, often going against the wishes of the public as represented by the national government.

The Labour viewpoint is that the government has neglected the state education system:

1) By using education as <u>a battleground in the struggle between central and local government</u>.

2) By <u>not caring about the state system</u> since most cabinet ministers and senior civil servants send their children to <u>fee-paying public schools</u> and therefore have no personal interest in the quality of the state system.

3) By introducing <u>too many changes in the system that are badly thought out</u> and which ultimately do not work.

4) By <u>destroying the morale of teachers</u> by always blaming teachers for faults in the system.

5) By <u>starving the state education system of money</u> through reducing grants to local authorities for educational purposes. The lack of sufficient funds mean that:

- There is not enough money for <u>the number of teachers needed by schools.</u>

- Senior, experienced teachers are replaced by junior, inexperienced teachers <u>because they are cheaper</u>.

- <u>Class sizes get bigger</u> because there are fewer teachers and, as a result, primary school-children are taught in groups of more than thirty.

- There is <u>not enough money for books </u>and basic equipment.

- <u>School buildings are so run-down</u> that some are becoming unfit for use: the amount of money set aside for building and repairs has halved in the last ten years.

<u>This argument between the parties over standards in education was made more bitter through decisions by Tony Blair and Harriet Harman, as well as other senior members of the Labour Party, to send their children to selective, grant-maintained schools outside their local areas, thereby saying one thing about education while doing the opposite themselves!</u>

Cost of the National Health Service

There is a contradiction in all discussions about the cost of the NHS:

- On the one hand - All governments, but <u>particularly Conservative</u> governments, have been accused of making severe cuts in the health services.

- On the other hand - Governments have replied that they have actually been **increasing the funding** of the NHS for year after year, even though the existence of empty beds in empty wards and hospitals that have been totally closed down because there is not enough money for them.

The original idea of the people who set up the NHS was that it would become cheaper as it improved the health of the nation: the truth has proved to be the opposite.

<u>The more successful the NHS is in saving and prolonging life, and in finding and perfecting new medical techniques, the more expensive it is, with costs rising well beyond the rate of inflation.</u>

- <u>Over 90% of all drugs in use by the 1990s were unknown fifty years ago</u>. The more advanced and sophisticated the drug, the greater the cost of research and manufacture.

- Many thousands of <u>people who would once have died before they reached retirement age are now living to an advanced old age</u>. The cost of looking after the old and the cost of drugs required to keep people alive are a continuous and increasing drain on health service funds.

- New medical discoveries and surgical techniques such as transplant surgery are great advances in medicine and a triumph of the health service but they are very expensive to develop and provide.

It is estimated that, taking inflation and the cost of technical advances into account, the NHS budget needs to increase by at least **3%** a year just to cover the cost of caring for the old. As against that **3%**, recent research into NHS spending shows:

i) that the Labour government of 1974-79 increased spending on the National Health Service by **2.2%** a year.

ii) that the Conservatives between 1979 and 1990 increased their spending by about the same amount - **2.1%** each year.

Although successive governments have poured increasing funds into the NHS, that increase has always been a bit less than the amount of money really needed to keep the NHS at a steady level. In the words of the old saying, *'They are running hard just to stand still!'*

Ways to save the NHS money have been suggested.

- One possibility was **'hotel charges'**, by which a patient going into hospital would have to pay for bed, food and everything except medical treatment. These charges could be as much as £15 a bed a day.

- Another possibility was making it compulsory for everyone to have private health insurance, in the same way that car drivers are required to insure themselves.

In this way the costs of providing a health service could be transferred to the insurance companies.

For a time it was hoped that the re-organisations of the NHS that have been taking place since 1973, might help to lower the cost of the NHS. Unfortunately, <u>the most significant change brought about by reorganisation was a 30% rise in the costs of administrative and clerical staff</u>. In 1996 it was shown that the NHS bureaucrats had spent something like £500 million on computer systems that did not work.

The National Health Service and market forces

The policy of the last Conservative government was to change the NHS through a mixture of <u>competition, privatisation and the introduction of market forces.</u> When this process began in 1987 the NHS was almost bankrupt. Many health authorities did not receive enough money to last them a full year and they had to close hospitals, or parts of hospitals, between January and the start of the new financial year in April.

<u>With 4000 hospital beds empty, emergency wards and intensive care units were closed.</u>

The government created an **internal health market**.

• <u>General practitioners were made</u> **fund-holders** and given a budget out of which they could purchase services from hospitals and others, with any money left over going to their own practice.

- Hospitals became **self-governing NHS Trust Hospitals**, the equivalent of opted-out schools.

- Elected representatives were removed from health authorities and replaced by appointed quangos, so that local health authorities became purchasers of care services rather than providers.

The changes were imposed by Kenneth Clarke as Minister of Health, despite opposition from the British Medical Association for the doctors.

In other services:

- The provision of spectacles and dentistry are no longer free services for anyone except the old, the young and the means-tested poor.

- Prescription charges rose from 20p in 1979 to £5.75 by 1997, an increase forty times the rate of inflation, although 80% of prescriptions were free to children of school age, men and women over 60 and those receiving social security.

- The responsibility for looking after the old in residential care was moved from the hospitals to private residential homes, mostly paid for from the social security rather than the health budget. These private places were also means-tested and there was considerable resentment that old people who had carefully saved for a secure old age were now refused assistance because of their savings, while others had to sell the homes they had hoped to pass on to their children in order to pay for their own care.

Many people feared that these reforms in the NHS would lead either:

i) to the <u>privatisation of the NHS</u>

or

ii) to the formation of <u>a two-tier service, with those patients registered with a fund-holding GP receiving preferential treatment compared with the rest.</u>

As the reforms continued and even Labour recognised that some changes were irreversible, the result seemed to be that the NHS would become a publicly-funded but privately-provided service.

In the 1990s there was talk of rationing, or **'priority setting'**. Under this, local health authorities draw up lists of medical conditions for which they will not provide unlimited treatment. Some rationed treatment is for minor operations such as varicose veins or wisdom teeth; others concern screenings or other preventative measures. But a few involve life or death decisions. In the summer of 1995 there was a big row over the decision by a local health authority that they would not pay for any further treatment for a child who was dying from cancer. The case opened up a new major issue:

<u>Should doctors try to keep alive the very old or the terminally ill, if the cost of doing so seems to be too much for their budgets?</u>

CHAPTER THIRTEEN

Constitutional Issues

There are various concerns about the British political system that have come to the surface in recent years and which can be grouped together as constitutional issues. These issues surfaced because it was felt that the British political system, as it has existed for so long, is <u>no longer right for the democratic needs of today</u>. In 1988 the feeling was so strong that a pressure group known as **Charter 88** was formed, to campaign for a number of reforms to the British constitution and political system. Main targets of Charter 88 include:

- <u>a written constitution</u>

  - <u>a Bill of Rights and Freedom of Information</u>

    - <u>devolution to Scotland, Wales and the English regions</u>

      - <u>reform of the House of Lords</u>

        - <u>modernisation of the Monarchy</u>.

Before all these, however, as a starting point, Charter 88 would like to see <u>a complete reform of the electoral system</u> used in Britain.

Most, if not all of these areas of reform were taken up by New Labour in the run-up to the 1997 election and the Blair government has, since then, proceeded to pass legislation giving effect to the reform programme. None of the reforms are complete and there are many who would argue that some of the reforms introduced are flawed in some way. Nevertheless, any consideration of the issue of constitutional reform must take into account just what has been achieved.

Electoral Reform

Third parties like the Liberal Democrats have protested for some time that the British electoral system of **first-past-the-post** is unfair to them in that they can <u>gain a large number of votes without winning many seats in parliament</u>. Also, it has to be considered that the Tory government that was first elected in 1979 and which dominated government throughout the 1980s and early 90s, won its initial victory on no more than about 40% of the vote - or, to look at it another way -<u> Britain had a government for 18 years that was disliked and unwanted by the majority of the people</u>.

Another result of the first-past-the-post system is that only two main parties have a real chance to form a government. And this sharp division of politics into two main parties means that parliament is run on a basis of **confrontation** instead of **cooperation**.

<u>A winner-takes-all electoral system produces a confrontational style of politics and gives control of parliament to parties with minority support.</u>

As a result of these doubts there are many people want to change the electoral system of this country. In 1991 the Labour

Party set up the **Plant Report** to look at the various systems that might be used in Westminster, European and Local Elections. Plant's proposal was that the present **simple majority system** (first past the post) should be replaced by either -

1) A **preferential vote majority system** - where voters list their preferences among the candidates and second choices are used until the winning candidate has the support of more than 50% of the voters

or:

2) By some form of **proportional system** - in which parliamentary seats are distributed between the parties in the same proportions as the electorate voted for those parties.

The arguments for reform

- are mostly to do with fairness.

- In the present system there is no relationship between votes cast for a party and the seats gained by that party. If you divide the number of votes cast for a party by the number of seats gained by that party in the 1992 General Election: -

  - it took **57,979 votes** to elect a **Conservative MP**

  - **32,326 votes** to elect a **Labour MP**

  - **103,586 votes** to elect a **Scottish Nationalist MP**

  - and **115,958 votes** to elect a **LibDem MP**.

- In every election more people vote **against** the party winning the election than vote **for** it. In the 1997 Election the Labour Party won **419** of the **657** seats - a massive landslide victory, but that was with only **44.5%** of the national vote. Labour had a massive majority, even though **55.5%** of the electorate voted for other parties. No government since the end of the war in 1945 has won an election with a vote of over 50% of the electorate.

- Because the system works against all candidates who do not have a clear chance of winning, electors tend not to vote if they think their vote might be *"wasted"*. This works against, not only third parties like the Liberal Democrats or Greens, but also minority groups like **women** or **ethnic minorities**. Parties do not select candidates from these minority groups because the party chiefs do not think the electors would vote for them.

The arguments against reform

- include such points as:

i) losing the link between constituency and MP

ii) the difficulty of understanding proportional representation (PR).

The main argument is that PR would mean more parties getting into Parliament and all governments having to become **coalition governments**. Arguments against PR are therefore usually concerned with the faults of coalition government.

- Government in Britain is supposed to be continuous but, with Parliament elected by PR there would be a delay of

204

several days or even weeks <u>while politicians negotiated on who would form the government.</u>

- **Coalition** governments are weak because smaller parties in the coalition can withdraw support at any time and bring a government down.

- Small parties with very little support can gain more power than they deserve because their support is keeping the government in power and they can demand special favours in return for that support.

- Electors vote for one party's manifesto rather than another. To form a coalition government one party would have to drop some of its own proposals and accept ideas from other parties. The result is a government with a programme that was <u>never placed before the electorate</u> and which <u>no one had ever actually voted for</u>.

- It would be impossible for governments to introduce major social changes because parties would have to compromise on their proposals. It is probable that reforming governments such as the Labour Government of 1945 or the Thatcher Government of the 1980s would not have existed under proportional representation.

Reforms by the Labour government

The Blair government has done more than any preceding government to introduce a reformed electoral system. Since 1997 a variation of the <u>additional member system</u> has been adopted for elections to the Scottish Parliament and Welsh Assembly, while <u>regional lists</u> were used in the 1999 European elections. The Scottish Parliament began to look at the possibility of proportional representation in Scottish local elections. Forms of <u>a preferential vote majority system</u> have been suggested for London's elected mayor and strategic authority. And finally, a commission on electoral reform led by Lord Jenkins has proposed that a form of the <u>Alternative Vote</u> should be used for Westminster elections and the government is committed to holding a referendum on the voting system preferred by the electorate before the next general election.

A Bill of Rights and a Freedom of Information Act

All Britons are proud of the rights they have as British citizens but in fact there has been <u>nothing</u> written down <u>which might guarantee them those rights. The Law is full of rules telling them what they</u> **cannot do**, <u>but there is nothing to tell them what they</u> **can do**. If the law is vague about this then it is often left to a judge to decide whether someone has acted *"within their rights"* or not. Many people feel that we should not depend on judicial decisions in this way but that our rights should be set down as written law <u>so that everyone clearly knows what they can and cannot do.</u>

There is a sense in which Britain has had the equivalent of a Bill of Rights for some time. In 1948 the Council of Europe (*N.B. nothing to do with the EU*) drew up the **European Convention on Human Rights**, which has its own **European Court and Commission of Human Rights** in Strasbourg. In 1950 Britain was one of the first countries to sign the Convention but Britain failed to accept the Convention

206

and, if any British citizen wished to appeal to the Convention they had to suffer the expense, delays and difficulties of acting through the court in Strasbourg. After 1997, however, one of the early acts of the Blair government was to incorporate the European Convention into British national law, permitting judgments based on the Convention <u>to be made and granted by British courts</u>. That acceptance of the European Convention meant that the UK could now claim to have a Bill of Rights.

Alongside the need to know our rights there is a need to know what is happening and <u>what is being done in our name by government, local authorities, the courts, the police and so on</u>. Events like **the Scott Report** show how much of government is carried on in secret and people generally feel that a lot of things they need to know are deliberately being kept from them; often simply <u>so that the government should not be embarrassed</u>. There is a feeling that government should be **open**, with everything clearly explained, except in cases where making information available would <u>endanger national security or breach personal privacy</u>.

The government has always resisted a **freedom of information act** on the American model and there is still a lot of information that is kept secret. But some progress was made some years ago when legislation was passed to prevent government bodies holding secret files about individuals. Any records that might be kept - such as the medical records made by doctors, or academic records kept by schools - may be confidential, but the person about whom the records are kept has a right to see what has been written about them in those records.

In opposition the Labour Party always promised that they would enact some form of Freedom of Information legislation when they gained power. But, although that promise remained a declared objective of the government elected in 1997 any legislation was very slow in emerging. When, in 1999, the Labour government finally produced a <u>Freedom of Information Bill</u> it was widely criticised as being inadequate. There may be concessions to openness but Britain remains a secretive society.

Devolution to Scotland, Wales and the English regions

The British public outside London tends to think of the government as <u>South-East England running the rest of the country</u>. This is particularly true of Scotland, which was a separate country with its own parliament and government until 1707, or Wales, which has its own language and culture. It is even true for regions of England like the North or South-West who see London as <u>a distant place which does not understand the problems of the regions</u>. Plans to devolve government to Scotland and Wales have been in the air for some time and a first attempt to devolve power was made in 1979, only to be thwarted by failed referendums. In 1997 the newly elected Labour government renewed their plans for devolution and successfully pursued them in referendums which produced favourable responses - overwhelmingly so in Scotland but little more than adequately in Wales. Consequently devolved governments were established:

Devolution for Scotland

A Scottish parliament of 129 members, 73 of them elected according to the <u>first-past-the-post</u> system in Westminster-like constituencies, and **56** <u>top-up members elected proportionately</u> for regional seats based on former Scottish Euro-constituencies. The Scottish parliament has powers over all decisions previously taken by the Scottish Office. Scottish MPs themselves elect a **Chief Minister** who is in effect <u>the Scottish prime minister and head of government</u> and who effectively replaces the Secretary of State for Scotland. The Scottish parliament has been granted the right to pass primary legislation in the form of **tax-raising powers**, including the ability to vary income tax <u>plus or minus 3p</u> from the UK level.

With Scotland granted a devolved government the question arises as to what should be done about altering the balance of representation in England. This is what is known as the **West Lothian Question** because it was first asked by Tam Dalyell when he was MP for West Lothian. The West Lothian Question is:

<u>If Scotland got its own parliament or assembly but kept its 72 MPs at Westminster, would it be fair that English MPs would have no say over Scottish legislation while Scottish MPs could debate and vote on English legislation?</u>

One suggestion is that the number of Scottish constituencies at Westminster should be reduced. However, this could be a serious issue for the Labour Party since so many Labour MPs have Scottish constituencies that any Labour government has to rely on Scottish MPs for it majority!

Welsh Devolution

Takes the form of a 60-member Assembly elected in May 1999 with **40** members elected by first-past-the-post and **20 additional members** elected proportionately for **5** former euro-constituencies. The Welsh Assembly has **no** legislative or tax-raising powers and the Welsh Secretary continues to have some influence. However, the Assembly administers a £7 billion grant, replacing quangos with elected administations. 9 of the 45 main quangos were replaced immediately, the others followed later. The Assembly has smaller committees to oversee its various responsibilities and there are safeguards to protect the north and rural areas from domination by Cardiff and the South.

Reform of the House of Lords

Everyone has been agreed that the Lords is in need of reform for some time, even the Lords themselves. But no one has been able to agree on the nature of the reform. The last attempt to reform the Lords in 1969 failed because of an alliance between Enoch Powell, on the right of the Conservatives, who did not believe in reform, and Michael Foot, on the left of the Labour Party, who felt the Lords should be abolished not reformed.

- As a first step to reforming the House of Lords, the government has **removed the right to vote from hereditary peers, restricting the powers of the Lords to life peers and a token 92 transitional hereditaries.** The government claims that replacing hereditary peers by life peers is a significant reform. But, since life peers are appointed by the prime minister rather than elected by the people, they are not much more democratic than hereditary peers.

- One alternative that has been suggested is that the second chamber could be abolished altogether. But the present House of Lords does serve a useful function in dealing with uncontroversial but time-consuming work on behalf of the House of Commons. A single chamber parliament would find it very difficult to deal with the volume of work.

- Another alternative, favoured by the more democratically-minded is that the Lords could be turned into an elected chamber but, simply to make it another elected chamber, with constituencies and party organisations, could end up by merely duplicating the Commons. Careful thought would have to be given as to how and why members of the second chamber would be elected and they would have to have a completely different function and composition to that of the Commons.

The Monarchy

There is a great deal of discussion about the monarchy at the moment and many people are now willing to put forward the idea of Britain becoming a **republic**. The criticisms of the monarchy are of two types:

- There is a belief that the monarchy is out-of-date and has no place in a modern democracy. Along with the House of Lords, the monarchy represents the rigid class structure of Britain and <u>all the unfairness and snobbishness of any system based on heredity</u>. The problem with royalty is like the hereditary peers' ability to hold up the workings of parliament - it is **"power without responsibility"** and the ability to influence political decisions <u>without having to answer to the public</u> for their actions.

- Even among people who believe in the monarchy there are those who believe that the present royal family has gone too far:

    - the royals have become too involved with <u>scandal in the tabloid press</u>.

    - too many of the younger members of the royal family have had <u>marital problems that have ended in divorce</u>.

    - few people criticise the Queen but there are seen to be <u>too many hangers-on, more distant relations who are paid an allowance from public money for doing very little</u>.

    - too many royals have been happy to appear on television and in the tabloid newspaper gossip columns, <u>destroying the air of remote mystery</u> that used to surround royalty and turning them into soap opera stars.

There is <u>a growing republican movement</u> in Britain that would like to see the monarchy abolished and replaced by **an elected president**, as other countries in the Commonwealth have done. There is no intention of getting rid of the present queen <u>but she would not be followed by another monarch on her death or abdication</u>.

There are possibly even more people who feel it is probably best to have a non-political figure as symbolic head of state and do not want to get rid of the monarch, but who would like to see reforms that would make the monarchy more democratic or would remove the uneasiness caused by recent scandals. Possible actions might be:

- **Remove the royal prerogative** - including things like declaring war or dissolving parliament. These powers are in the hands of government ministers and not the monarch, but they use the royal name to do things without consulting parliament. If the royal prerogative were taken away the government would have to consult parliament before doing anything.

- **Disestablish the Church** by giving up the royal title of Head of the Church of England, which is no longer a realistic position to hold in the modern world.

- **Maintain the present monarch** and the immediate royal family but end public payments to cousins and more distant relations. There have already been cuts in the **Civil List** (money granted by parliament to support the royal family), and the Queen is now paying income tax. But some people feel that this could go much further.

- **Remove the automatic right** of the Prince of Wales to succeed to the throne. If it is felt that the troubles of the prince's marriage should rule him out from ever becoming king, then it should be possible to by-pass him in favour of one of his sons.

A Written ~~Ros~~ titution

Many, if not all, of these reforms would make it virtually obligatory that Britain should look again at the question as to whether the country should have a written constitution.

- A *Bill of Rights* could certainly form the major part of a written constitution, as is the case in the United States.

- *If the monarchy were reformed* by withdrawing the royal prerogative, there would have to be a written set of rules to replace what is currently done on a traditional basis.

- *Devolution of power* to parts of the United Kingdom will probably require written regulation of the relations between the various devolved regions at some stage. All federal systems like the United States require constitutional laws to govern relationships between the states and although the British political system is not yet federal it is acquiring some federal characteristics.

The important thing to remember about constitutional reform is that something as complicated as the British Constitution cannot be played with. Change in one area affects change in another. Charter 88 did not draw up its list as a series of alternatives, they wanted all the reforms mentioned - as one all-in package, clarified by being written down.

214

CHAPTER FOURTEEN

Issues of Society

Law and Order

Traditionally, law and order has been an issue that favoured the Conservative Party; Labour being thought to be *"too soft"* on the criminal. Whenever opinion polls asked the voters which party they thought was best equipped to deal with the issue of law and order, those questioned almost always chose the Conservatives. In 1994, however, this changed and opinion polls began to show a regular lead for Labour over the Conservatives on the issue.

This change in people's ideas was largely as a result of the way crime figures had increased over the years that the Conservatives were in power.

- In **1979** there were **4,833** crimes reported for every 100,000 people in the population.

- In **1993** there were **10,614** crimes reported per 100,000.

  - this is an increase of **127%**

- Over the same period, **clear-up rates** (the percentage of crimes solved) fell from **41%** to **26%**.

The Conservative answer to problems of law and order has always been to crack down harder on the criminals. The answer in the 1990s was the **Criminal Justice Bill**, introduced in December 1993, which promised no fewer than 27 *"get tough"* measures, including:

- removal of the **right to silence**.

- **six new prisons** to be built (to be privately run).

- **doubling maximum sentences** for young offenders.

- heavy **restrictions on granting bail**.

- powers to act against **'new age travellers'**,

   those holding **'rave' parties**,

   and those **protesting over animal rights**.

Other measures introduced by Michael Howard as **Home Secretary** included

changes in the caution given by police to suspects

granting the right for police to carry arms (including guns)

automatic life sentences for certain crimes such as rape

a reduction in the amount of money available to compensate the victims of crime.

The Home Secretary's plans were very popular with the **Conservative Party Conference**. But one or other of them were criticised by large sections of the community, including:

- **Civil rights groups** who disliked changes to the **'right**

to silence' and measures taken against <u>new age travellers, rave parties and protest groups.</u>

- **Judges and magistrates** who did not like to see <u>the right to fix sentences</u> taken away from them, and what they saw as even more <u>pressure on overcrowded prisons.</u>

- **The police** who were given extra work without any real increase in numbers, who saw new guidelines they did not like and who did not want to be armed.

All three groups of critics, including the **Lord Chief Justice,** united in telling the Home Secretary that <u>it is not severe sentences that will deter criminals but the risk of being caught. The concentration should be on helping the police with clear-up rates.</u>

This helped the **Labour Party** which believes that an increase in crime is the result of <u>social conditions such as unemployment, poverty, bad housing and poor education.</u> For Labour the problems of law and order cannot be solved by harsher penalties <u>intended merely to punish and deter.</u> Alongside a tough policy in the courts there should be:

- **Increased police presence** on the beat and in the community, so as to prevent crime happening in the first place.

- **A social policy** to remove things like poverty and badly planned housing estates <u>which cause criminal activity.</u>

Tony Blair, before he became leader, summed up Labour's policy on law and order: Labour, he said, would be:

Tough on crime and <u>tough on the causes of crime.</u>

The attitude towards law and order typified by this statement of Tony Blair helped to change public attitudes to Labour's role in the law and order debate. This was very much reinforced by Jack Straw's performance as Home Secretary, in which office he has shown himself to be as traditionally authoritarian as any Tory Home Secretary. Representatives of Old Labour have been much more critical, feeling that the Blair government has perhaps gone too far in adopting the tough attitude to crime.

The Police

The real questions about the police are:

Who is in charge of the police?

and

Who investigates complaints against the police?

Back in the 19th century the public was afraid of a national police force controlled by the government, like there was in many European countries. It was thought that a national police service could be used by an authoritarian government to suppress the people. For that reason the only police force that is directly controlled by the Home Secretary is the Metropolitan Police in London. Elsewhere in the country, the police are funded and run by local government, through what was once called the **Watch Committee** and is now usually known as the **Police Authority**.

Many critics, especially on the left in politics, believe that there are those who would like to see the police having a greater control over society. During the Miners' Strike of 1985 there was cooperation between police forces and <u>a national incident room</u> set up with information fed through <u>a centralised computer system</u>. Civil liberties groups claimed that this was intended to be the beginning of a national police force with secret records kept on all British citizens.

The control of the police by politicians in local government leads to regular conflict. The way it should work is that:

The Police Authority is responsible for all policies related to policing.

The Chief Constable and his or her officers is responsible for all police operational matters.

This means, however, that:

<u>Police Authorities are always complaining about Chief Constables who make policy decisions without consulting their Authorities.</u>

<u>Chief Constables are always complaining about Police Authority politicians who interfere in operational matters without knowing anything about how the police work.</u>

The other cause of conflict is the problem of complaints against the police and allegations of wrong or corrupt practices. There have been many examples of bad practice in recent years, from widespread corruption in the Metropolitan Police to allegations of rigged and faulty evidence made against the West Midlands Crime Squad. However, the policy is that complaints against the police are investigated by the police themselves. This leads to suspicions by the public as to how far the reports of enquiries into the police can be trusted and how far there have been cover-ups to shield the guilty.

<u>The demand is for an independent investigator, like the Ombudsman, who can look at all accusations against the police without being biased in any way.</u>

The Role of Women in politics

In Britain women have only had equal voting rights since 1928. Yet women have been campaigning for equal status with men for centuries. And, even though women have got the vote they are still under-represented in parliament. 52% of the population are women but they represent less than 10% of MPs. The question as to why there are so few women in parliament is obviously a major political issue.

- <u>Many men do not really believe that women can do the job</u>. The joke on the television satire show, "*Spitting Image*", that Mrs Thatcher was a man in drag was only repeating a general belief that <u>a 'real' woman could not make a 'proper' prime minister</u>.

- **The selection committees** who choose election candidates for local constituency parties <u>do not believe that electors will vote for women candidates,</u> so they do not choose women candidates.

- The House of Commons is like a man's club, working unsocial hours that do not suit a woman's life style and without there being even simple facilities for women, like women's toilets, in the Palace of Westminster.

- If a woman tries to have a family **and** a career she will probably not enter politics until she is much older than a male politician. This gives her less time in the House of Commons to gain experience for ministerial office.

- In the Labour Party selection as a candidate is easiest if you are sponsored by a trade union but the union movement is dominated by men - and men get chosen.

- Even if a woman is selected as a candidate she is unlikely to be chosen for a safe seat, they are kept for those candidates whom the party really wants - usually men!

- Even when a woman is selected as candidate, is elected to parliament, and becomes a minister, it is unlikely she will get one of the top ministerial jobs. **Women are chosen to be ministers of health or education or welfare.** They are unlikely to be finance ministers or ministers for foreign affairs or ministers for trade and industry, **those are seen as being "men's" jobs**.

- The Labour Party tried to even up the balance by insisting on **all-women short-lists** when constituencies were choosing candidates. But some men took a constituency party to court and all-women lists were declared to be illegal. As a result the party began to treat the policy of all-women lists with extreme caution.

- One product of positive discrimination in the Labour Party was the 1997 election when the number of women Labour MPs rose from 37 to 101, known as *"Blair's Babes"*.

Even though women may not be properly represented in parliament, women have always been active in politics. For nearly 200 years there have been campaigns on **women's issues** such as <u>divorce, married woman's property, the right for women to be educated and to work in the professions</u>. Women have often been involved in community action and <u>women were allowed to take part in local government long before they were allowed to vote in parliamentary elections</u>. In Britain there are nearly **three million women** in organisations like the **Women's Institute** and other women's clubs, all of which are involved in influencing local and national government on a range of political issues.

There has been a steady growth in support for the **Women's Liberation Movement** since the 1960s covering a wide range of issues from <u>Battered Wives</u> to <u>Abortion Clinics</u> to <u>Peace Camps</u> to <u>Support for the Miners</u>. Despite the **Equal Opportunities Act** and legislation on equal opportunities, women still tend to be treated unfairly at work compared to men. But women's groups have found that **European Law** is much more favourable to women and many groups have <u>appealed successfully for better and fairer treatment in the European Courts</u>, on things like maternity leave and benefit, equal pension rights and job security.

Racism and Race Relations

Since the 1950s Britain has increasingly become **a multi-cultural society**. Large numbers of non-white immigrants from Commonwealth countries like the West Indies and the Indian sub-continent came in search of work during the 1950s and 60s and became established in Britain, creating communities of non-whites who were born in Britain.

There have always been groups of immigrants in Britain who have suffered from discrimination and prejudice by the native British. Over the centuries Flemings, Irish, Jews and Blacks have been persecuted because they act, speak and look differently from the native British. Racial feeling is worst for the non-white immigrants because, while immigrants of European origin blend in with time, non-whites remain very visibly different.

Non-white Britons suffer certain disadvantages:

Housing - they are forced into **ghettoes** in areas of poor housing in the inner cities, over-crowded and with poor facilities.

Employment - the immigrants originally came to do the jobs that no one else would do and it remains true that blacks are mostly employed in low-paid, unskilled manual jobs. It is also true that, in a period of high unemployment, blacks are more likely to be unemployed than whites. The trade unions have not done much to help because one of the causes of racial prejudice is the fear that "*the immigrants are going to steal our jobs*".

223

<u>Education</u> - non-whites do not do well in education, partly perhaps because of language difficulties but also because of prejudice by teachers who have <u>low expectations</u> of how well black students can do.

<u>Police harassment</u> - rightly or wrongly, non-white young men, particularly Afro-Caribbeans, claim that the police are always 'picking on' them. This again is because of <u>the high visibility of non-whites</u> but there are certainly racists in the police force. Unfortunately <u>reaction against police pressure often leads non-white youths into crime</u>, allowing the police to believe that they were right all the time.

<u>Racism</u> - there are groups, especially in white working-class areas, who are associated with parties like the **National Front** and the **British National Party** which are openly and violently racist in their policies, using violence against members of ethnic minorities and their property. This racism affects all parts of society, even the major institutions of society: one product of the debate over the murder of Stephen Lawrence and the police handling of the case, was the report of an enquiry that found that **"institutionalised racism exists in the Metropolitan Police"**.

<u>Working Class problems</u> - many of the problems of non-whites, like bad housing and unemployment, are <u>problems common to the working class of whatever colour</u>. However, it is true to say that non-whites are disadvantaged because of both their race and their class - <u>they are doubly disadvantaged</u>.

The main political parties are supposed not to be racist. Both Labour and Conservative governments have introduced <u>equal rights legislation to prevent racial discrimination</u> and there is a **Commission for Racial Equality** to monitor race relations. However, both parties have also introduced anti-immigrant legislation and it is often said that the Conservative government in iis last few years was too harsh in its policy of deporting illegal immigrants. The Labour government of 1997 did not prove much different, however, and Jack Straw's proposals on immigration policy were so harsh that they triggered a major backbench revolt among Labour MPs.

Just as is the case with women, there are non-white MPs and non-whites in important positions, but not in anything like the numbers that would be expected from the number of non-white British citizens. There are those who claim that the situation can only be put right by **positive discrimination**.

The Environment

Concern for the environment has been growing for some years now, but the turning point in political terms came in the 1989 elections to the European Parliament. In that year the Liberal-SDP Alliance was breaking up and support for the **'third party'** transferred to the **Green Party, who got 15% of the vote**. Because of the British electoral system, no Green Party candidate was elected, even though the British Green vote was higher than in those other European Green parties who did elect MEPs. However, the high Green vote persuaded the other parties that environmental issues were important to the electorate, and from then on all political parties produced policies on the environment and claimed to be "*greener than the Greens*".

The main environmental concerns are:

- **Pollution** of the air, water and soil.

- **Conservation** of fossil fuels (coal and oil).

- **Preserving** natural plant and animal life and the areas where rare species live.

- **Control** of toxic and nuclear waste.

The main British parties all have environmental policies and some 'green' legislation has been passed, such as favourable tax rates for lead-free petrol. All the same, the environment as an issue is one:

- where people put more trust in **direct action through pressure groups** than they do in the promises of political parties.

- where the **most important legislation comes from Europe** rather than the Westminster parliament.

- Membership of environmental pressure groups such as **Green Peace** and **Friends of the Earth** is greater than membership of some political parties. It is particularly strong among young people who want to become involved in politics but who do not trust politicians.

- In 1995 the European branches of **Green Peace** defeated the Shell Oil company and several European governments over the disposal of a North Sea oil-drilling rig, *Brent Spar*, at sea.

- Environmental pressure groups have mobilised thousands of protesters, often middle class men and women not usually associated with protest movements, to fight against <u>engineering schemes that threaten the</u> <u>environment</u>, like the Newbury by-pass or the second runway at Manchester Airport.

- The **European Community** has <u>issued directives to</u> <u>control pollution</u> by high levels of <u>sulphur dioxide, lead</u> <u>in exhaust gas, carbon dioxide and ozone.</u>

- Following instructions from Europe, the Ministry of Agriculture launched the **Habitat Scheme** which gives government grants to farmers who set land aside from farming and <u>who agree not to use chemicals and other</u> <u>polluting substances on land which supports wild life</u>.

- The European Community <u>held up the privatisation of</u> <u>water in Britain</u> until they were satisfied that the supply of water was properly regulated.

- In 1993 <u>Lancashire County Council successfully</u> <u>prosecuted the British government in the European</u> <u>Court of Justice, for failing to clean up three bathing</u> <u>beaches in the county</u>.

- The **European Commission** is far more ready to hear complaints about the environment than the British government. <u>On average there are 125 complaints to</u> <u>Europe each year about British offences against the</u> <u>environment</u>.

The Media

Most concern over the media is expressed about the press, and about **the tabloid press** in particular. And there are two main issues concerning the tabloid press:

1) **The ownership of the press** and its concentration into too few hands.

2) **The amount of bias shown by the press** and the degree to which the press can manipulate public opinion and influence political events.

The main worry over ownership is the influence of Rupert Murdoch. Owning the *Sun* and the *Times*, reaching about **30% of daily newspaper readers**, and the *Sunday Times* and *News of the World,* with about **37% of all Sunday newspaper readers**, Murdoch is the most powerful and influential newspaper owner in Britain. He also owns **B-Sky-B television**. There were laws to prevent him owning a share of a tv station in Britain, but Murdoch claims that since Sky-tv is broadcast by way of the **Astra Satellite** which is registered in Luxembourg, the tv station is European and not British.

British newspapers are very partisan in their politics and they are overwhelmingly in favour of the Conservatives. Of the daily newspapers at the time of the 1992 election support was:

Conservative	Labour
(70% of readers)	(27% of readers)
Sun	*Daily Mirror*
Star	*Guardian*
Daily Mail	*Financial Times*
Daily Express	
Daily Telegraph	
Times	

Most *Sun* readers normally vote Labour, in spite of the *Sun*'s support for the Conservatives. In fact, in the 1992 election 24% of those voting Labour read the *Sun*. But support for Labour is weak enough for the readers to be influenced by sensationalised reports by *Sun* journalists. In the 1992 election campaign there were a number of stories intended to attack Labour in general and Neil Kinnock in particular. The two most famous headlines were -

Nightmare on Kinnock Street

and

If Kinnock wins today will the last person to leave Britain please turn out the lights

The scare stories were enough to make **8%** of *Sun* readers switch their votes from Labour to Conservative. If all the scare stories in the other tabloids had the same effect, that explains why there was a sudden switch to the Conservatives at the last minute, letting them win the election in spite of opinion polls predicting a Labour victory.

- The *Sun* itself said, on the day after the election - "**It's the Sun wot won it**."

- Margaret Thatcher told the editor of the *Daily Express*, "*You won it.*"

- Lord McAlpine, Tory fund-raiser, claimed that the editors of the tabloid press were "*the real heroes of the election campaign*".

- Even Neil Kinnock, in his resignation speech, said that the tabloid press had <u>won for the Tory Party what the Tory publicity campaign could not win for itself</u>.

<u>All the evidence suggests that the media have more importance for political behaviour than might be expected.</u>

Before the 1997 election Tony Blair and New Labour actively wooed the Murdoch press and, in the event, the *Sun* and other tabloids either openly or tacitly supported Blair. It can be argued that they did so because they wanted to be on the winning side and they recognised that Labour was going to win that election no matter what anyone did. Nevertheless, New Labour was helped rather than hindered by that change of attitude on the part of the press.

CHAPTER FIFTEEN

Foreign Affairs, Defence and Northern Ireland

Foreign Relations

There was a time when the conduct of relations with foreign countries was one of the most important duties carried out by the government. Since the end of the Second World War in 1945, however, this has become less true for Britain.

- Although Britain still has a permanent place on the **United Nations Security Council**, as one of the five victorious allies in the Second World War, Britain is no longer counted as being a leading world power. Ever since 1945, the position previously held by Britain, and other European countries like France, was surrendered to the super-states like the United States of America and the Soviet Union.

- Since 1945 Britain has lost the <u>British Empire</u>, as most of the former colonies have won or been given independence. Sometimes, however, the remains of the Empire can involve Britain in disputes with other countries. This was the case with the Falkland Islands and the war with Argentina in 1982. And former colonial

links with Kuwait involved Britain in the Gulf War with
Iraq in 1990.

Britain's relations with the rest of the world are now largely
decided by the international groups to which Britain belongs.
The more important of these groups include:

The European Union which since Maastricht has agreed to
follow a common foreign and security policy. Britain became
involved in Bosnia and the former Yugoslavia as part of an EU
initiative. The EU has its own defence organisation, the
Western European Union, of which Britain is a member.

The Commonwealth which is made up of countries that
were formerly part of the British Empire, although the 'British'
was dropped from the title some years ago. The Commonwealth
heads of government meet at regular intervals to discuss world
affairs. All countries within the Commonwealth are equal and
Britain is no longer regarded as the leading country, although
the Queen is thought of as Head of the Commonwealth.

The North Atlantic Treaty Organisation (**NATO**) was
formed during the Cold War to defend the West against the
Soviet Union. It is still a powerful international defence
alliance with a headquarters near Brussels and, although it
lost a lot of its reason for existing with the end of the Cold War,
it did play a major role in the Bosnian and Kosovo conflicts in
former Yugoslavia.

The Organisation for Economic Co-operation and
Development (**OECD**) was set up to help rebuild Europe after
the war and has since grown into an association of developed
industrialised nations who cooperate on matters of trade and
the economy. Within the OECD there is also the **G7 Group of**

<u>Nations</u> which represents the seven leading capitalist countries, who meet at regular intervals to discuss mutual problems.

Most foreign contacts now - <u>including state visits by the Queen abroad, or by foreign heads of state to this country</u> - are for the purposes of <u>promoting trade</u> with foreign countries and the *commercial section* is often the most important part of British Embassies abroad. Britain also gives a lot of aid to **Third World Countries** and the government includes a **Minister for Overseas Development**. But that aid often takes the form of helping to pay for British firms to undertake development work in the countries concerned.

It is a well-known fact of British political life that the British electorate is completely uninterested in foreign affairs and the government's conduct of foreign relations has no effect on voting behaviour. The only exception to this is that, during a pre-election period, it is usually thought to be good for the prime minister's image to be seen as an international statesman and visits are made to capital cities like Washington and Moscow.

Defence

Defence is no longer so important an issue, as it was even as recently as the 1987 general election. This is because the main issue concerning defence - the possession of **nuclear weapons** - has lost much of its importance since changes in Russia during 1989-90 brought <u>the end of Communism, the break-up of the Soviet Union, the fall of the Berlin Wall, the re-</u>

unification of Germany and the ending of the Cold War between East and West.

After the start of the Cold War in 1946 Britain's defence concentrated on the alliance with America and membership of NATO. NATO policy centred on the deployment of nuclear weapons and, while it was hoped that Britain could depend on the American alliance, it was still very important for successive governments that Britain should maintain its own, independent nuclear deterrent.

There were many people in Britain who did not want the nuclear arms race, in which countries competed with each other to see how many nuclear weapons they could make and possess. Pressure groups like the **Campaign for Nuclear Disarmament (CND)** tried hard to persuade all countries to give up their nuclear weapons but they particularly wanted Britain to give up its independent nuclear weapons as an example to other countries. This one-sided surrender of nuclear weapons was known as **unilateral disarmament** and was much favoured by the Labour Party; being official party policy at times in the 1980s. Many senior Labour politicians, like Neil Kinnock, had been or were members of CND.

Unilateral disarmament was not popular with the electorate and during election campaigns the Conservative Party would make a great deal of fuss about how the Labour Party would throw away the country's weapons and leave Britain defenceless. The defence issue was one of the main reasons for Labour's poor performance in the elections of 1983 and 1987, particularly when Mrs Thatcher claimed to be in favour of strong defences and quoted the Falklands War to show how strong she was.

234

Defence seemed to lose its importance overnight. The end of the Cold War in 1989 meant that there was less risk of war with the Soviet Union and this brought what was known as the **'peace dividend'**, which was a way of saying that <u>money that was once spent on defence could now be spent on other things</u>. Normal defence with conventional non-nuclear weapons was still important, as was seen in the Gulf War of 1990. But nuclear defence was the issue which concerned the electorate and, without the threat from the Soviet bloc, the British electorate rapidly lost interest in the importance of unilateral disarmament.

<u>In 1987, 35% of the electorate said that defence was the most important issue to influence the way they would vote.</u>

<u>By the time of the 1992 election, only 3% of the electorate named defence as an important issue.</u>

Northern Ireland

The issue of Northern Ireland is very complicated and the situation there changes almost daily. It is also unusual in being an issue about which there is basic agreement between the main parties in the Westminster parliament. Northern Ireland is not therefore an issue like the others we have been discussing, since there is no argument between the parties and it is not likely to affect voting behaviour in mainland Britain.

In 1920 the southern counties of Ireland became an independent **Irish Free State** within the British Commonwealth. In 1949 the Free State cut its links with

Britain and became the **Republic of Ireland**. In these settlements it was established that <u>there were six counties in Northern Ireland which were dominated by a Protestant majority</u>, compared to the rest of Ireland which was devoutly Catholic. Since the Protestants of the north were apparently ready to fight to remain British the southern Irish had to accept the partition of Ireland. <u>The Province of Northern Ireland was formed</u>, with its own parliament at **Stormont**, <u>which continued to be part of the United Kingdom.</u>

<u>Irish nationalists never accepted the partition of Ireland</u> and they continued to struggle to re-unite Ireland. That struggle was partly political but there was also the *'armed struggle'* in which the **IRA** used shootings and bombings against the British and Stormont governments. Not all the nationalist and Catholic population of Northern Ireland supported the IRA but they were all hostile to the political system imposed by Stormont, which manipulated the political and electoral system so as to <u>maintain the Protestant majority in power</u> and which <u>discriminated against the Catholic minority</u> in areas like housing, employment and the law.

In the 1960s, encouraged by the success of the American civil rights campaign, conducted by the blacks under Martin Luther King, a largely middle-class and Catholic-led movement in Northern Ireland began to campaign for Stormont to concede basic **civil rights** to the Catholic minority. Moderate nationalist, left-wing and Catholic opinion formed a new political party, the **Social and Democratic Labour Party (SDLP)**, which was to represent the rights of the minority in a non-violent and democratic fashion. The civil rights movement also created an important political figure for the minority population in **John Hume**, later to become leader of the SDLP.

The Northern Ireland government made many concessions to the Catholic community but Catholics saw these concessions as being too little, too late, while any concessions at all were seen as being too much by the Protestants. The civil rights movement continued, with marches and protests, but they were increasingly met by a Protestant back-lash. The old Unionist Party - that had ruled at Stormont since 1921 - split, with less moderate leaders like William Craig and **Ian Paisley** emerging. More seriously, the exclusively Protestant special police force known as **the B Specials** acted very violently against Catholic protesters. With the **Royal Ulster Constabulary (RUC)** unable to contain the situation, Stormont called for military help from London and British soldiers were sent to the Province in 1969.

At first the British soldiers were welcomed by the Catholic community, who saw the army as coming to save them from the B Specials. But the Stormont government increasingly called on the army for help, until the British army became firmly associated with Stormont in the eyes of most Catholics. At the same time an extreme nationalist grouping replaced the old IRA, which had largely given up the armed struggle. This was **Provisional IRA**, and its political wing, **Provisional Sinn Fein**. The **Provos**, as they were known, represented themselves as defenders of the nationalist/republican/Catholic community against what they called the 'British colonial occupiers'.

For three years, faced by increasing violence from the IRA and other paramilitary groups like the INLA, and with counter-violence coming from the army and RUC, the London and Stormont governments argued over civil rights and control over security. In 1972 the Heath government ended the

237

devolution of Northern Ireland with the abolition of Stormont and <u>the imposition of</u> **direct rule** <u>from London</u>. In 1972 the Troubles really started, with the IRA and other republican paramilitaries <u>waging war on the British presence in Ireland,</u> and conducting <u>a terrorist bombing campaign against British</u> <u>targets in mainland Britain and Europe</u>. To complicate matters <u>the Unionist/Protestant/loyalist community also produced its</u> <u>paramilitary gangs</u>. Alongside the so-called armed struggle there was also a civil war of **sectarian killings** in which Protestant paramilitaries murdered Catholics and vice versa.

After 1972 there was continuous violence and repeated attempts to reach agreement in a political settlement. Each time there seemed to be hope of an agreement one side or the other would refuse to co-operate:

- A **Power-sharing Executive** set up in 1974 was brought down by a Protestant workers' strike.

- A **Northern Ireland Assembly** in 1982 was hampered from the start by the refusal of the Unionist parties to share power with the Republican parties. As a result it was boycotted by Sinn Fein and the SDLP.

- **The Anglo-Irish Agreement** of 1985 between the London and Dublin governments was a major advance because Dublin recognised that <u>there could only be</u> <u>change in Northern Ireland with the consent of the</u> <u>majority</u>. The agreement provided for regular meetings between British and Irish ministers and a permanent staff of <u>British</u> **and** <u>Irish</u> civil servants based at Stormont to help negotiate agreements on **cross-border disputes**. The agreement was totally opposed by the Unionist parties who refuse to allow that Dublin has any

238

<u>a whole.</u>

- A serious **Peace Process** began in the second half of 1994 with an <u>IRA cease-fire,</u> followed by similar announcements from the loyalist paramilitaries. However, the British government and Unionist parties refused to take part in talks with parties such as Sinn Fein, as long as paramilitaries kept their weapons and could threaten to re-start the violence if talks failed. Sinn Fein, for the IRA, stated that they were willing to enter talks as equal partners, but <u>to give up their weapons would be like admitting defeat</u>. They would do nothing that might suggest surrender. In late November 1995, only days before President Clinton was due to arrive in Northern Ireland, a deal was fixed. A **twin-track** approach would be adopted by which the arms issue was separated from the question of talks. Negotiations for talks would continue on one track while the arms question would be examined separately by an **international** and **independent** commission under a former US Senator, George Mitchell.

- <u>The IRA cease-fire ended in February 1996 with a bomb set off at Canary Wharf in London</u>, Sinn Fein blaming the British government for bad faith and delaying tactics. Other bombs followed in Germany and Manchester and it began to look as though the peace process was breaking down. During the Protestant **marching season** in the summer of 1996 there were confrontations and renewed violence between the two communities.

- On 15 July 1997 the entire province was horrified when 'loyalist' gunmen dragged Catholic Bernadette Martin from her Protestant boyfriend's home and shot her dead. 3 days later Gerry Adams and Martin McGuiness for Sinn Fein urged the IRA to call a ceasefire and, on the 19th, that ceasefire was restored. In September, the government accepted that the IRA ceasefire had lasted long enough for Sinn Fein to be admitted to the peace talks. Sinn Fein then agreed to the Mitchell Principles, foreswore violence and accepted that weapons would have to be surrendered.

- On Good Friday 1998 agreement was reached that there was to be an elected **Northern Ireland Assembly** of **108** members, <u>elected by PR in 6-member constituencies</u>. The legislative powers of the Assembly would be weighted to <u>prevent domination by the Unionists</u>. The executive body of the Assembly is a **'cabinet'** of **12** members, including <u>first minister, deputy first minister and ministers for finance, health, education, agriculture</u> etc. The Assembly is also to set up and supervise a North-South body to deal with cross-border issues. Efforts were to be made to settle outstanding issues such as the decommissioning of arms and the accelerated release of paramilitary prisoners.

- On 22 May 1998 there was a referendum in both Northern Ireland and the Republic intended to approve the <u>Good Friday agreement</u>. Despite a great deal of opposition, the referendum was a massive success for democracy with an <u>81% turnout</u> and a <u>resounding endorsement of the Peace Deal through **71% voting 'yes'**</u>. The results were reflected in similar figures in the

Republic of Ireland. A month later came the elections to the Assembly and once again the electorate ignored those who wanted to reject the deal. As a result of the elections David Trimble became first minister of the Assembly, with Seamus Mallon of the SDLP as his deputy. One significant result was to give sufficient votes to Sinn Fein to entitle them to two ministerial positions - meaning that Gerry Adams and Martin McGuinness are likely to be given places in the devolved government.

242

PART FOUR - APPENDIX

PRACTICAL ADVICE ON GCSE ASSESSMENT

Assessment of the GCSE Politics course consists of two components:

A written examination paper, with four compulsory questions, worth 80% of the marks

and

A coursework assignment, between 1500 and 3000 words long, worth 20% of the marks.

The written paper is offered on two tiers:

Tier F (Foundation) - aimed at grades G up to C

Tier H (Higher) - aimed at grades D up to A*

Obviously this book cannot tell you how to pass the examination but it can give you some hopefully helpful advice on what you are likely to be asked to do and how best to tackle it. The first thing to do is **to read this book carefully**, taking particular care to <u>learn the political terms and ideas</u> that are printed in bold or underlined. Although you will need to learn rather more than the basic information that is included in this book if you want to do well, particularly by keeping up-to-date with the news, <u>there will be nothing in the written paper that is not mentioned somewhere in this book</u>.

The Written Paper

The paper is divided into four questions, each of which is then sub-divided into three, four or five part-questions. The four questions are compulsory but the part-questions will often offer you a choice. The four questions each represent part of the syllabus:

Question 1 is entitled **What is Politics** - it is associated with Part One of this book and is largely concerned with <u>individual participation in politics</u>.

Question 2 is entitled **Decision Making** - this covers things like <u>legislation, the working of parliament, government - local and national - and the importance for decision making of parties, political groups and the European Union</u>. Most of the information can be found in Part Two of this book.

Question 3 is entitled **Accountability** - this deals with the way in which the decision makers have to answer for their decisions. It covers topics like <u>the scrutiny of legislation, ministerial responsibility, the ombudsman, parliamentary committees and non-elected bodies like quangos and agencies</u>. Again, most of the information can be found in Part Two of this book.

Question 4 is entitled **Political Issues** - this corresponds to Part Three of this book and can deal with any political topic that can be regarded as an issue. But the question will be particularly concerned with those <u>issues which influence voting behaviour</u>.

Each question is provided with a generous amount of stimulus material. <u>This should be read very carefully</u> because:

- the actual answers to some simple questions can be found in the stimulus material.

- the stimulus material can provide clues to how you should answer the questions.

- the right answer can sometimes be worked out from the material provided.

In the 1996 examination a lot of candidates did less well than they should have done because they did not read the material provided carefully enough. For example, question 1 (b) [in tier P, 1 (a) in tier Q] asked *'Which government agency is responsible for looking after old buildings?"* On the opposite page was the statement *'The society will appeal to English Heritage for Eastwood Manor to be listed as a building of historic interest'*. If candidates had read the material carefully there should have been an easy mark there for everyone. But, as it happened, less than half the entrants managed to find the answer *'English Heritage'*.

On the other hand, in Question 3 candidates did make good use of the material provided. They were asked to name the government department responsible for the agency Milk Marque. They did not necessarily know which department it was but they were able to see on the opposite page that there is a Department of Agriculture responsible for farming and food, and most were able to work out that milk has to do with farming and food and that the Department of Agriculture was therefore the answer.

The stimulus material is very wide-ranging because the questions are not supposed to tie you down to one narrow part of the syllabus. For example, in the 1996 examination, Question 1 had stimulus material showing:

246

a) the agenda for the AGM of a local historical society which had a councillor, an MEP and a JP among its officers.

and

b) a newspaper cutting about moves to demolish an old building, the demolition of which was to be opposed by the historical society.

This wide-ranging content allowed the part-questions in Question 1 to cover:

The political activities of clubs and societies (agenda, AGM, elections etc.)

Individual service to the community (councillor, MEP, JP)

The activities and processes of action groups.

What is meant by direct action.

Local government.

Each question is worth 20 marks but that is divided up between part-questions which themselves might be worth anything between 1 and 12 marks. You will be told how many marks each part-question is worth and you should pay close attention to this. The amount of time and effort you spend on a question should be related to how many marks it is worth. If a question is worth eight marks you will obviously need to spend twice as long, and write at least twice as much as you would if it were worth four marks. On one hand the answer to a question worth two or three marks does not call for more than a few lines but at the other extreme, an essay type of question worth up to twelve marks will call for at least a side or a side and a half in the answer book.

Part-questions will fall into one of several broad types:

- The first of the part-questions will often be simple right or wrong questions such as *'Which government minister is responsible for the Budget?'* Sometimes the answer might be in the stimulus material provided and sometimes you might be expected to remember it. But the answer is very short (*the Chancellor of the Exchequer* in this case) and <u>it will only be worth 1 or 2 marks</u>.

- Similar questions, but with more in the way of an answer expected, are **definition questions**, where you are expected to say what is meant by something. These questions will begin with a statement such as *'In your own words, explain what you understand by...'* or *'What is meant by...'* Then there will be a number of terms - as for example, *Chancellor of the Exchequer* or *Budget*. <u>You will not often be asked for just one definition but more probably will be asked for three or four</u>. Be very careful in reading the question to make sure that there is not a choice involved. Very often you will be asked *'Explain what you understand by **three** of the following terms...'*, followed by a list of five or six terms. Do not simply answer the first three but read through all of the terms and <u>choose very carefully which ones you are most certain about</u> and answer those. <u>Do not waste time by answering more questions than you are asked to do</u>.

- In short questions, like definition questions, <u>pay special attention to the marks available</u>. If you are asked what is meant by three terms and there are three marks for

248

the answer then you are being given one mark each for three simple definitions. If, on the other hand, you are asked to define three terms and there are six marks available then <u>you must assume that there are two marks being given for each answer</u>. For each one you must give an adequate definition for one mark and then an example or some further information to gain the second mark.

- Beware of comparison questions. Examples on the 1996 paper included the *'difference between Green Papers and White Papers'*, the *'differences between a select committee and a standing committee'* and the *'difference between the Minister in charge of a government department and the Chief Executive of a government agency'*. Remember that you are only going to get full marks for questions like these if you answer both parts of the question - <u>just one definition is not going to get you more than one mark</u>! In the question about the Minister and Chief Executive, students had no trouble writing about ministers because a lot of information was included in the stimulus material, but a few students only got one mark because they said nothing about chief executives.

- There will always be part-questions that call for a longer answer and, for the benefit of those who are good at writing essays, these part-questions, worth between eight and twelve marks, can be answered as essays. Usually there will be a choice between two or three possible essay titles.

There are two points to remember when answering essay-type questions:

1) Always answer the question that has been asked <u>and **not**</u> <u>the question that you would like to have been asked</u>. There is a tendency for students to prepare the answer to a question they are expecting and then to write that answer, whether or not they are asked the question. For example, in the 1996 Q examination paper the question was asked '...*describe the part played by Europe in the British decision-making process.*' There were several candidates who had prepared an essay on the European Union - listing member countries and describing institutions like the Commission. These candidates saw the word '*Europe*' in the question and insisted on writing their prepared answer. Their answers were very good and they were factually quite correct but <u>they had nothing to do with the decision-making process,</u> <u>did not answer the question and did not get many marks.</u>

2) <u>Always read the question very carefully.</u> Sometimes the question will include hints as to what should be included with words like '*...in your answer you should mention...*' Other questions will ask for more than one thing and you need to be sure that you give as full an answer as possible. For example, in the 1996 Q examination paper, part-question 1 (d) asked '*What is meant by the term 'direct action' and how effective do you think it is? In your answer you should give examples from recent campaigns.*' You should realise that the candidate was being asked for three things -

    i) a definition of direct action,

    ii) some examples of direct action

and

iii) an analysis of the effectiveness of direct action.

Most students could give reasonable definitions and were very good at examples but very few said anything about effectiveness beyond a brief statement like *'it was not very effective because the police stopped them'*. Yet, an idea of the importance of answering all parts of the question can be seen in the fact that, while the question as a whole was worth eight marks, <u>someone who did well in answering i) and ii) but did not attempt to analyse effectiveness would be lucky to get more than five marks</u>.

<u>The important thing to remember is to read everything very carefully - stimulus material and questions - and make sure you understand it quite clearly before you attempt to answer any questions.</u>

Read all the stimulus material provided very carefully.

Study the question until you are certain you know exactly what it is you are expected to do.

Coursework

Coursework is only worth 20% of the final mark but coursework marks can make the difference of a grade in the final assessment and the assignment should be taken seriously by all candidates. The syllabus defines the coursework assignment as **a report of between 1500 and 3000 words on a contemporary political development or issue.** The student's work is assessed on the ability to do four things:

- to show understanding of **political** information.

- to be able to collect political information from a **variety of different sources** using **more than one method of investigation**.

- to be able to use that information in **creating an argument** and **drawing a conclusion**.

- to be aware of the relevance and accuracy of information; including showing **an awareness of any faults** in their own work and knowing how the work done could have been improved **if done differently**.

Choosing your topic:

- All proposed coursework submissions have to be approved by the Examination Board but once a title has been approved it can be used again without having to ask for further approval. If your school, college or examination centre has entered candidates in previous years there will be coursework titles available that have already been approved. There is nothing to stop you using those titles again. The title you choose does not have to be different from that chosen by anyone else - if you like, the whole class or group can do the same coursework title, you can work together and co-operate in your investigations; **as long as the report you submit is your own work in your own words**.

- If you wish to do so, you can choose a new title for your coursework. Consult your teacher: he or she can advise you on the suitability of titles and on what sort of problems you might meet. There is nothing to prevent people like your teacher helping you with your assignment: in fact <u>teachers are expected to help and guide their students</u>. A record will be kept of the number of times you consult your teacher or anyone else; simply so as **to make it clear as to the extent that the assignment is all your own work**.

- **Your assignment must be political**. Every year students do not do as well as might be expected because they choose to write about something that is only marginally political. Examples are projects on *capital punishment, abortion, drugs, arming the police* and so on. Certainly, these subjects can all be political but <u>all too often coursework assignments with titles like this turn into sociological, historical or religious arguments</u> and the student scores very few of the marks that are available for **purely political** subjects.

- <u>Topics should be narrow rather than general</u>. As a student there is a limit to the amount of information to which you have access, just as there is a limit to the amount of information that you can get into a 3000 word report. You need to choose a title that can be tackled with your limited resources and which can be completed within the limited time and space you have available to you. Choose too wide a subject and you can get lost in your assignment.

- <u>Make sure that you will get the help you want and expect</u>. Do not put yourself in the position where you rely for help on people <u>who are too busy to spare any time for you</u>. Every year I dread the proposals of some students which say that they intend to base their work on replies

- the Prime Minister, the leader of the Opposition, leading figures in the political parties, a number of MPs and so on. I know very well that busy politicians like the Prime Minister <u>cannot possibly spare the time to answer every letter they receive</u>; and most MPs are so busy that they refuse to reply to letters from anyone <u>who is not one of their own constituents</u>. This is not to say that you should not attempt to write to these people: sometimes they can be very helpful. But, if you do get a useful reply, that is a bonus. <u>You should never be in the position where you are relying on these replies for the essential material you need in order to do your coursework.</u>

- <u>Try to concentrate on **local** matters</u>. It is usually much more interesting to tackle a topic that affects you and the local area you live in. If the subject of your assignment is local it is far <u>easier to get people to talk about it</u>; you have more chance of obtaining <u>comments from councillors and your local MP</u>; as a member of the public you are free to attend <u>meetings of your local council</u> where the matter might be discussed; people you interview or question are <u>more likely to have an opinion and to say something worth saying if it is a local matter</u>; and you will be able to get a lot of <u>useful information from the local newspapers</u>. There is no shortage of local issues to provide you with a suitable topic -

  - are there any local projects like a new road or the building of a supermarket over which pressure groups are protesting?

  - are there schools wanting to opt out of council control?

  - is there a parents' pressure group wanting a

children's crossing across a busy main road?

- are people worried about pollution from a local tip or do people want new leisure facilities provided?

- and so on.

<u>Even national political issues can be more easily approached from a local angle</u> -

- you could investigate the work of a local councillor or you could ask what your MP does for his or her constituents.

- ask how your local area is affected by Britain's membership of the European Union.

- what effect has de-regulation of the buses and privatisation of the railways had on public transport in your local area?

All the issues or questions mentioned above have been dealt with in above-average coursework assignments during the last two or three years.

• Above everything else, choose as your assignment **something you find personally interesting**. It is very difficult to work hard and finish your coursework if you find it dull or boring.

Methods of working and investigation

The syllabus requires your coursework assignment to be a personal investigation and says '*candidates are required to use a variety of sources and use different investigative techniques*

255

appropriate to the topic'. It would be possible to write a 3000 word report simply by going to the library, looking up the answer in a book and then writing a long essay. But, although books (known as **secondary sources**) are very useful <u>and have their place in your coursework</u>, a high level of marks is only available if you use one or more **primary source** (<u>things you observe or find out for yourself</u>).

<u>Primary sources can take many forms:</u>

- **Media audit**. This is when you analyse the content of newspapers or news broadcasts on radio and television. You can use the media as a source for a general topic and as one of the ways you find out the information you need. However, the media itself can be used as the subject of your assignment by comparing different newspapers for bias and accuracy. You can either follow one story over a period in one or more newspaper - *e.g. How do the tabloid newspapers cover the Northern Ireland peace process?* - or you can compare a range of different newspapers on one day - *how differently do they treat the main political stories? what evidence is there of political bias?*

- **Observation and case studies**. It is possible to learn a lot about certain political activities simply by <u>watching what goes on and then writing down what you have seen</u> and explaining what you understand about it. The obvious places for observation are the public galleries of councils, law courts, even Parliament. More useful and interesting is what is known as **participant observation**. This is when <u>you yourself are taking part in the activity you are observing</u>, and is particularly useful if you are a member of a pressure group. In the past I have seen some excellent coursework assignments:

from a member of a group protesting about fox-hunting; from an Asian student who helped the movement to stop a fellow-Asian from being deported by the Home Office; from a college student on the committee of her students' union. The question you have to ask yourself is <u>whether you should let the other members of your group know that you are observing them</u>. On the one hand you do not want to change the way people behave by letting them know they are being watched but, on the other hand, there are those who might say or do things that <u>they would not want reported, particularly if the group is involved in direct action or violent protest</u>.

- **Surveys**. These are the easiest forms of primary sources to use in your study because <u>you can tack a survey on to any assignment simply by asking a selection of people what their opinion is of the subject you are studying</u>. However, there are problems over the **sample** you use for your survey. Since you are limited in the number of people of whom you can ask questions, you have to choose <u>a small number of people to represent a much wider number</u>. <u>This is your sample</u>. As we know from the opinion polls this can lead to very misleading answers so you have to follow certain rules for selecting your sample:

  i) <u>Your sample should be representative</u>. People are of different ages, male and female, from different social groups and so on. If your sample was made up only of sixteen year-old males it would not be representative of the population of your town.

  ii) <u>Your sample should be as large as you can make it</u> because you want the opinions of as many people as possible to make your survey mean anything. Obviously you will be limited in the time you can spend on this, but you should aim for <u>at least a sample of 30, and preferably nearer 40 or 50</u>.

In order to make your sample representative and the size of your sample significant, you should limit the people whose opinions you are trying to discover. *It would be ridiculous for you to ask questions of your sample of 30 or 40 people and then claim that this represented the population of Great Britain!* <u>Keep it simpler</u> and think in terms of <u>opinion within your school or college, opinion in your club or society, or opinion in your neighbourhood</u>.

- **Letters, questionnaires and interviews**. These form the ways in which to carry out your surveys, although individual interviews can be used in case studies and an exchange of letters can provide material for any kind of assignment. Certain things should be kept in mind:

- Remember what has been said earlier <u>about writing to MPs, government ministers and other important politicians</u>. You might well not get a reply. (*If you really want to obtain information from an MP it is probably best to find out when your own MP holds a surgery in the constituency which you can attend*).

- <u>Prepare your questions beforehand</u>, make them very clear, short and political.

- **Do not** ask too many questions, ask questions that are unanswerable or ask personal questions that embarrass or are an invasion of privacy.

- Take care to keep your questions **free of bias** and beware of the slanted question which is intended to make the interviewee answer in a particular way.

- Ensure that your questions lead to <u>clear unambiguous answers</u> because you have to use those answers in writing up your report.

Presentation

- <u>Your report should be written up as neatly as possible</u>. If you have access to a word processor or a computer with word processing software so much the better, although it is not essential.

- Also useful, if not essential, would be the ability to <u>make a graphical presentation of your survey results</u>, or any other figures you are including, in the form of <u>graphs, charts and diagrams</u>.

- <u>Do not write too much</u>. You are only asked for a maximum of 3000 words, which is something like ten sides of writing on A4 paper.

- <u>Do not bother with fancy folders or ring-binders</u> - they only make your work bulky and expensive to send through the post. <u>Use a plain cardboard file or wallet-file</u>.

- Also, before handing in your work to be marked you should <u>remove all the material you have used to compile your report</u> - *leaflets, newspapers, hand-outs, completed questionnaires etc.* You should have made a note of where

259

you got your information in your report and you can keep all this material in case your teacher asks to see it. Otherwise it is just surplus to requirements.

- Your report **must** contain the following:

An introduction: In this you should say what it is you are intending to study and your reasons for choosing this topic. You should say how you intend to set about studying the subject, the methods you intend to use and what you expect or hope to find out or prove.

The central argument: Try to organise the information as well as possible, leaving out any unnecessary information and explaining any findings from your own surveys or research. Include any graphs, tables or illustrations where possible. If you quote from any of the books you have used, put the author's words in quotation marks and put the author's name and the title of the book in brackets after the quote.

Analyse your own work: Be critical of your own work. If you think you could have done better if you tried again say where you think you went wrong and how you would do it now given a second chance. You can usually get as many marks for showing that you know where you went wrong than you could get for getting it right first time. On the other hand, if you think your work was successful, do not be afraid to say so and why. This criticism of your own results is tied up with -

The conclusion: Sum up what you have found out. In particular, point out just <u>how you have done what you said you would do in the introduction</u> and <u>how far what you have discovered bears out what you expected or hoped to discover</u>.

Bibliography: You should add <u>a list of all those books you have used in your assignment</u>, whether you have quoted from them or not. To do it properly you should give the title of the book, the name of the author or authors, the name of the publisher and the date it was published. Also <u>list any newspapers, magazines, pamphlets or leaflets you have used</u>. You might also choose to <u>acknowledge people who helped you, whether personally or by letter</u>.

Remember in your coursework that it is not what you find out but the way in which you find it out. You are being tested on how well you can carry out a political study.

Whether in the written examination or in your coursework just do your best to show the examiner what you 'know, understand and can do'. Nobody is trying to catch you out and there are no trick questions.

Just do your best and the best of luck!

INDEX